Vedic Astrology Secrets for Beginners

The Complete Guide on Jyotish, Nakshatras, and Hindu Astrology. Ancient Teachings for The Soul, Relationships, Self-Esteem & Spiritual Growth.

Manjula Tara

© Copyright 2020 by Manjula Tara. All right reserved.

The work contained herein has been produced with the intent to provide relevant knowledge and information on the topic on the topic described in the title for entertainment purposes only. While the author has gone to every extent to furnish up to date and true information, no claims can be made as to its accuracy or validity as the author has made no claims to be an expert on this topic. Notwithstanding, the reader is asked to do their own research and consult any subject matter experts they deem necessary to ensure the quality and accuracy of the material presented herein.

This statement is legally binding as deemed by the Committee of Publishers Association and the American Bar Association for the territory of the United States. Other jurisdictions may apply their own legal statutes. Any reproduction, transmission, or copying of this material contained in this work without the express written consent of the copyright holder shall be deemed as a copyright violation as per the current legislation in force on the date of publishing and subsequent time thereafter. All additional works derived from this material may be claimed by the holder of this copyright.

The data, depictions, events, descriptions, and all other information forthwith are considered to be true, fair, and accurate unless the work is expressly described as a work of fiction. Regardless of the nature of this work, the Publisher is exempt from any responsibility of actions taken by the reader in conjunction with this work. The Publisher acknowledges that the reader acts of their own accord and releases the author and Publisher of any responsibility for the observance of tips, advice, counsel, strategies, and techniques that may be offered in this volume.

TABLE OF CONTENTS

INTRODUCTION	7
CHAPTER 1: WHAT IS VEDIC ASTROLOGY	11
ASTROLOGY: LOOKING TO THE STARS FOR ANSWERS	12
THE VEDAS, HINDUISM AND VEDIC ASTROLOGY	14
VEDIC VS. WESTERN ASTROLOGY	15
THE PURPOSE OF VEDIC ASTROLOGY	19
LEARNING TO USE VEDIC ASTROLOGY	21
CHAPTER 2: THE HISTORY OF VEDIC ASTROLOGY	25
THE ORIGINS OF VEDIC ASTROLOGY	26
IMPORTANT TEXTS	27
VEDIC ASTROLOGY AND THE REST OF THE WORLD	28
CHAPTER 3: THE VEDIC BIRTH CHART	31
THE DIFFERENT CHARTS	33
FINDING THE POSITION OF THE SUN AND MOON	37
FINDING THE PLANETS' POSITIONS	42
SIGNIFICATORS (*KARKA*)	43
EXALTATION AND DEBILITATION	43
CHAPTER 4: THE PLANETS (GRAHAS)	47
UNDERSTANDING THE PLANETS AND THEIR POSITIONS	48
THE SUN (RAVI OR SURYA)	50
THE MOON (*CHANDRA*)	52
MERCURY (BUDHA)	55
VENUS (*SHUKRA*)	58
MARS (KUJA OR MANGAL)	60
JUPITER (GURU OR BRIHASPATI)	63
SATURN (*SHANI*)	65
RAHU (NODE OF THE MOON)	67
KETU (NODE OF THE MOON)	69
PLANETARY CONDITIONS	70
COMBUSTION OF PLANETS	71
RETROGRADE PLANETS	73

Chapter 5: (The Zodiacal Signs) — 75

- Dualities and the Zodiac — 77
- Triplicities and the Zodiac — 77
- Quadruplicities and the Zodiac — 79
- Aries: Cardinal Fire (*Mesh*) — 81
- Taurus: Fixed Earth (*Rishabh*) — 82
- Gemini: Mutable Air (*Mithun*) — 82
- Cancer: Cardinal Water (*Karka*) — 83
- Leo: Fixed Fire (*Simha*) — 84
- Virgo: Mutable Earth (*Kanya*) — 85
- Libra: Cardinal Air (*Tula*) — 86
- Scorpio: Fixed Water (*Vrischika*) — 87
- Sagittarius: Mutable Fire (*Dhanus*) — 88
- Capricorn: Cardinal Earth (*Makara*) — 89
- Aquarius: Fixed Air (*Kumbha*) — 90
- Pisces: Mutable Water (*Meena*) — 92

Chapter 6: The Houses (Bhavas) — 95

- Trinities of the Houses — 97
- Cardinal, Fixed, and Mutable Houses — 98
- First House: Ascendant (*Lagna or Tanu Bhava*) — 99
- Second House (*Dhana Bhava*) — 103
- Third House (*Buddhi Bhava*) — 106
- Fourth House (*Bandhu Bhava*) — 109
- Fifth House (*Putra Bhava*) — 112
- Sixth House (*Ari Bhava*) — 115
- Seventh House: Descendant (*Yuvati Bhava*) — 118
- Eighth House (*Randhra Bhava*) — 121
- Ninth House (*Dharma Bhava*) — 124
- Tenth House (*Karma Bhava*) — 128
- Eleventh House (*Labha Bhava*) — 132
- Twelfth House (Vairagya Bhava) — 136

Chapter 7: The Lunar Mansions — 141

- Aswini: The Horse Goddes — 142
- Bharani: The River of Souls — 142
- Krittica: The Star of Fire — 143
- Rohini: The Red Goddess — 143
- Mrigashira: The Star of Searching — 143
- Ardra: The Tear Drop — 144
- Punavasu: The Light Bringer — 144
- Pushya: Nourishment — 144
- Ashlesha: The Coiled Serpent — 145
- Magha: The Forefathers — 145
- Purva Phalguni: The World Tree Goddess — 145
- Uttara Phalguni: The Marriage Goddess — 146
- Hasta: Skilled Activities — 146
- Chitra: The Jewel — 146
- Swati: The Wind God — 147
- Vishakha: The Moon of Power — 147
- Anuradha: The Moon of Friendship — 147
- Jyeshtha: The Wisdom Crone — 148
- Mula: The Root of All Things — 148
- Purva Ashadha: The Moon of Early Victory — 148
- Uttara Ashadha: The Moon of Later Victory — 149
- Shravana: The Moon of Listening — 149
- Danishtha: The Drummer — 150
- Shatabhisha: The Divine Healer — 150
- Purva Bhadrapada: The Fire Dragon — 151
- Uttara Bhadrapada: The Dragon of the Deep — 151
- Revati: The Moon of Splendor — 151

Chapter 8: The Significance of Vedic Astrology — 153

- Vedic Astrology and Naming Children — 154
- Vedic Astrology and Karma — 156
- Vedic Astrology and Matchmaking — 157
- Vedic Astrology for Self-Awareness — 162

Chapter 9: Vedic Astrology Today — 165
- Modern Uses of Vedic Astrology — 166
- Science and Vedic Astrology — 169
- The Planets and People—Are They Really Influential? — 170
- Advanced Vedic Astrology Degrees — 172

Chapter 10: Introduction to Stargazing — 175
- How to Stargaze — 176
- Objects in the Sky — 178
- Discerning Stars and Planets — 180
- The Zodiac vs. Constellations — 182
- Getting Started — 183

Chapter 11: Utilizing Vedic Astrology — 185
- Transit Charts and the Planets — 186
- Aspects and Transit — 187
- Applying the Information — 191

Conclusion — 197

Description — 203

INTRODUCTION

We have looked to the stars for millennia. Humanity has looked to the stars to find all of the answers for ages, looking to the ways that the stars would move, tracking the patterns of the celestial bodies to make sense out of what happens around us. They have been used to navigate. They've been looked to as explaining the truth about people and personalities. The stars have been seen as something for the gods, a way for us to understand the universe. They've been used to represent the divine.

Even today, we look at the stars. Have you ever heard of astrology? We're often quick to say that we're a Virgo or a Gemini, but what does that really mean? And, is it really accurate to discuss in the first place? Is it possible that the stars actually can influence what we become just by their placement at the time of our birth?

Vedic astrology, commonly also referred to as Hindu or Indian astrology, is tied directly to this concept. It recognizes that at the exact moment of your birth, there is a sign that ascended from the horizon. This sign is directly related to you and who you are and what you will do with your life. Your sign is defined at that very moment of your birth. It is a much more open system—it looks at the stars to define the life that you will have. However, it is more than just looking to the life that you will have—it looks at your ability to have free will at the same time. In Vedic astrology, you take a look at both fate and free will both at the same time. Now, while that may sound like it is an oxymoron, we will be taking a look at what that means in this book.

Vedic astrology is shrouded in mystery. It is a point in which science and art intertwine, and it allows for us to look toward the stars for answers. Vedic astrology is believed to be the word of God, translated and recorded by the people of the past. It involves tracking the stars and planets as well as works to create insight into our life and fate. It is something that many people believe in, and for a good reason—it is a great way to interpret the world around you.

Within this book, we will delve into the idea of astrology, starting to demystify the vast field little by little. The purpose of this book is to create a sufficient foundation in Vedic astrology so that you can begin to understand the concepts and apply them yourself. As you read, you will discover the true meaning of the Planets above you have to offer. You will discover how to begin deciphering the stars, the Planets, the Moon, and the Sun so that you can begin to use them to understand the world around you.

Astrology is a vast field, where our understanding of science and math coincides with our ability to think and rationalize about the future and our understanding of life. Though some reject it as a pseudoscience, it is even possible to get degrees in Vedic astrology, with the study of it being incredibly deep. Founded upon the Vedas, this interpretation of astrology is believed to be more exact than the Western counterpart for reasons that we will address. There is an emphasis on the moon over the sun, and because the Moon changes its sign more rapidly, it can usually be seen as more accurate.

We will first delve into the idea of Vedic astrology, along with the rich history that is paired with it. A solid understanding of the most basic concepts is the foundation that you will need to continue throughout the book. From there, you will discover other information that can be of the utmost use to you, such as the history of how Vedic astrology came to be, as well as what it looks like today. We will take time to delve into the Planets, learning their meanings when it comes to the astrological reading, as well as the Zodiacal signs that are applied. We will learn about the Houses, Lunar mansions, and more.

INTRODUCTION | 9

From there, after we've taken a look at the key concepts, we will spend some time going over the significance of Vedic astrology and the meaning that it has to the people who use it. We will learn to understand these concepts so that we can better apply them where they matter the most. From there, we will take a look at Vedic astrology and what it has become today. We will take a look at how it is used, and also why science is so hesitant to acknowledge it.

We will then take a look at how you can begin to stargaze yourself, so you can begin to look for the signs in the stars yourself, and finally, we will tie that into understanding and utilizing Vedic astrology for yourself as well. The hope is that by the time you read the last chapter, you will feel competent enough to start to use these techniques for yourself. Little by little, and with enough experience, you will get there, and you will realize that you can begin to interpret the stars yourself.

It might seem like a lot at first, but rest assured that you are more than capable of learning to implement these tools if you are willing to put in the time to do so. Whether you're curious about the topic or ready to delve into something deeper, this book is for you to provide you with plenty of beginner's information so that you can make your own judgment calls. As you dive in, remember to keep an open mind and really start to absorb the information. You may realize that it resonates with you more than you thought it would!

Now, let's get to work. Let's start to go over the ins and outs of the information that you will need to get moving. You can learn to understand other people with ease. You can learn to better recognize their own patterns. And, all you have to do is work to memorize some information and start interpreting it! It's not nearly as difficult, foreign, or mysterious as you may initially think. Though the forces work in mysterious ways, you will find that there are plenty of ways that you can learn everything yourself.

CHAPTER 1:
WHAT IS VEDIC ASTROLOGY

Astrology is one of those topics where some people love it, and others choose to hate it. Some believe in it passionately while others are convinced that it's nothing but hogwash and attempts at vague predictions that will have to be true to some degree. How can it be accurate if you look at a horoscope and read, "You'll get some good news today!"? What would warrant that good news in the first place? Who's to say that the good news that you receive is that you've won the lottery or been offered your dream job as opposed to being told that the person in front of you paid for your latte, or discovering that the sandwich meat that you were buying was actually half off that day?

Despite the naysayers, one thing is for sure: People around the world believe vehemently that astrology works. We love being able to explain the unexplainable, and astrology helps us do exactly that. It gives us some extra context to our lives, allows us to see and feel in control of what is going on.

Within this chapter, we are taking a look at everything that you will need to know to get that foundation of knowledge out of the way. We will first look at what astrology in general is, understanding how it works. Then, it will be time for us to dive into information about the Vedas and how it has relevance to Hinduism. From there, we will define Vedic astrology, as well as contrast it with the Western rendition. Finally, we will wrap up this chapter with information about both the purpose of Vedic astrology and how you can begin to learn how to use it. This will be that basis that you will need heading into the rest of the book so that you will have the necessary context.

If this sounds like a lot to pack into one chapter, that's because it is. However, this is all information that is absolutely essential to help yourself better understand the context that you will need. When you look to the stars, you will find that you will have just as many questions as answers, and this chapter will help you begin to understand them.

This chapter is just the beginning. As you read throughout the book, you will realize that the information that you have gained is going to continue to compound upon itself. It will continue to change, grow, and to reflect differences that you will need to address as well. However, with time and effort, you can do it. Learning to read astrology does not require you to go to college, though there are degrees that exist out there. It doesn't require you to be an expert at math either—all you need is the background knowledge and the experience to begin to apply it over time.

Now, let's take a look at some of the most fundamental information. Don't be afraid to take things slowly, to ease yourself into understanding these concepts. There is a lot here in this book to take in, and it can be intimidating. However, don't let yourself get discouraged—you can make the progress that you want!

ASTROLOGY: LOOKING TO THE STARS FOR ANSWERS

For as long as we've recorded history, we've looked up to the sky to get answers. We've looked to the heavenly bodies above in hopes of making sense of the world around us, wondering what they do to influence ourselves and how we behave. We've looked at the positions of the Planets, the stars, the sun, and the Moon in hopes of being able to understand what we are doing at the moment. The positions at one's moment of birth are believed to be influential—they are believed to directly impact the destiny of an individual.

Astrology provides us with a tool that we can use to better interpret the world around us. We can use it to better understand ourselves and those around us just by being able to see the stars above. We use it to define the world that we live in and to begin to understand behavior. It lets us better understand the character of those that we interact with, and it creates a way for us to discuss what we observe. It is used to recognize that there are influencing factors that exist outside of people, and those influencing factors can be greatly beneficial to understand.

However, it is important to recognize that your astrology reading, any birth charts or horoscopes, or anything else does not decide your fate directly. However, you will be able to interpret the world, the karma that goes into it, and more all because you will be able to recognize the signs that exist around you.

If you've ever said something like, "Oh, I'm just stubborn that way; I'm a Taurus," then you're already familiar with the idea behind astrology. Yes—your horoscopes that you may have read online are created with the concepts of astrology backing them. They are based on your Zodiac signs—which were determined based on the position of the Sun in relation to the constellation presiding at that point in time.

We've focused on astrology as a species for a long while—we've cared to see how what we do influences everything else. We've looked at why we do the things that we do and what can come of it as a result.

Within astrology, we look at the position of the Sun, as well as the Planets. Every person also has a sing for the Planets and the Moons. We have Houses and birth charts to understand as well. Our character is impacted by all of this—it determines our personality, and we have found ways to look at the stars for more information. Astrology itself can be thought of in several different ways—it can be broken down to use for predictions. It can impact the study of relationships and more. There is so much that you can learn about astrology just by being able to see the patterns.

THE VEDAS, HINDUISM AND VEDIC ASTROLOGY

Some of the most significant texts in the Hindu religion are known as the Vedas. Coming from the Sanskrit word for knowledge (Veda), they are a compilation of four texts that are recognized as influential. There are four in particular: The Rigveda, Yajurveda, Samaveda, and Atharvaveda. Each of these is broken down into four more subdivisions. First, there are the Samhitas, the mantras, and benedictions that are offered. Next comes the Aranyakas, the rituals and ceremonies that go into the religion. You will also see the Brahmanas—commentaries upon the aforementioned rituals. Finally, there are the Upanishads, the texts that discuss knowledge, meditations, philosophy, and more.

The key with the Vedas, as opposed to the other religious texts found in Hinduism, is that they are sruti. This means that they are what is heard as opposed to being smrti—what is remembered. Effectively, the Vedas are considered to be authorless—they are superhuman and are the revelations of what the ancient sages who recorded them had heard during and after their own meditations. Since the second millennium BCE, they have been passed down through the generations through oral methods, utilizing chants, recitations, and other tools to remember them in order to pass them on. While some parts are still recited orally, namely the mantras, the Vedas have since been recorded in a written form.

Throughout the Indian philosophies and Hindu denominations, there are several different interpretations of the Vedas. However, the vast majority of them acknowledge that the Vedas is a collection of sacred texts that ought to be followed. These texts are recognized and defined, as being necessary to better understand life and to better choose the right behaviors to live a harmonious life.

The Vedas are believed to be that direct knowledge from the sages, which they heard by the divine. They provide us with information that is transcendental; it tells us of the truths of the universe in order to allow us to live a better-rounded, balanced life so that we can be certain that we are proceeding with the most harmonious lives that we can.

Jyotish, another name for Vedic astrology, is believed to be a part of the Vedas. In particular, during this Vedic period of time, astrology was deemed to be essential and integral; we looked to it to help us to decide what to do and how to determine what is right. For this reason, Jyotish became its own designation, separate from astronomy (Ganita) and astrology (Phalita). We will be getting into more detail about this time in the next chapter, however. For now, let's just acknowledge that this period of time mattered immensely.

Vedic astrology is the oldest form that exists today. It is still practiced in ways that are nearly identical to how it once was. It is deemed so influential that the calendars used in India still rely upon the Lunar mansions and Vedic astrology. In this form of astrology, you will see that there are 12 signs (Rashis), 27 Lunar mansions (Nakshatras), 16 types of horoscopes (Shodashvarga), and several Planetary periods (Dasas). As you can see, there are several different elements that come into play here, with many others also existing. There are the yogas—the predefined combinations of Planets to understand one's life. There are so many different topics that come into play here, and you will need to have a solid understanding of them all if you hope to begin implementing Vedic astrology.

VEDIC VS. WESTERN ASTROLOGY

With the aforementioned information in mind, you will discover that Vedic and Western astrology are both quite different from one another. First, you will probably notice that the charts are completely different. Western astrology is based upon a circle while the Vedic chart is square. You will also notice that the charts will appear to be aligned differently. This means that if you are a Taurus in Western astrology, your sign may be something entirely different. This is because the Western astrology looks at which constellation the Sun is in rather than looking at which sign is rising. Vedic astrology looks to the rising sign rather than the Sun sign, and that can generate very different horoscopes than what you may be used to.

This difference, however, makes Vedic astrology more precise. When you use Vedic astrology, you look at the position of the sky in that moment of your birth, and that becomes directly linked to you. Because the Earth is always moving, the sky can look very different based upon whether you were born in the morning or the evening. Because you will get a very personalized reading based on your location and time of birth, it is believed that your Vedic chart will be far more reliable when it comes to making predictions toward the future.

This difference in accuracy matters greatly for people—the way that you look to the Planets will show that there are very different reactions to be had. In Western astrology, there are longer periods of time in any sign, and that can make them vague and difficult to maintain. When you look at Vedic astrology, however, the specificity and the true uniqueness based on date, time, and place, means that your reading will be highly accurate. You will see the past, present, and future all intertwined together, and there is very real power to be gained in doing so. This power matters immensely—it is good for you to be able to use so that you can successfully interpret the karma of the past, how that karma will come to fruition in the future, as well as your own current personal tendencies. You will be able to tell what your own personal reactions are more likely to become as well, meaning that you will be able to know yourself better than you might have thought. In reflecting over the tendencies, you will probably realize that there is far more to it than you thought. You might realize that your personality actually has more nuances that you might have never considered until interpreting your own charts, and that's okay—this is meant to share all sorts of information with you so that you will know yourself better. It is meant to give you that insight, and if you find that it does so, you will be in a great position—you will realize that this has served the right purpose after all.

In Vedic astrology, the times of life events are able to be seen through Planetary time cycles—these are the dashas, and there is no Western counterpart. Vedic astrology is oftentimes the preferred method due to the fact that it is deeper and more accurate; when Western astrologers take the time to study the Vedic astrological charts, they tend to convert on their own.

In particular, when you use Vedic astrology over Western, you will get two distinct differences. In particular, you will get a better view of the individual's tendencies in regards to their karma, a topic that we will get into in more depth later within this book. Additionally, you will get to identify the tendencies that are much more likely to manifest for those individuals as a result of what you can see and understand. These details provide far more information than what you can get out of Western astrology.

Beyond just that, you can expect to see some differences in the astronomy as well. As a note, astronomy looks at the celestial bodies themselves to understand how they move. Astrology starts to interpret those results. There are some key differences that you can see between Western and Vedic astrology that you must address—in particular; they work differently. Western astrology utilizes what is known as a Tropical Zodiac, while the Vedic Zodiac is Sidereal. This is important to note: It means that the constellations will align differently. In Sidereal astrology, you will note that there are 27 constellations or star groups. Aries is the first Zodiac sign, and it aligns with the constellation Aswini. In Tropical Zodiac, however, the point where the Sun passes the Earth's equator is that defining start point. The Tropical Zodiac rotates—it is a turning Zodiac with a fixed point of Aries between the Earth and the sun's rotation, whereas the Sidereal focuses on gentle, subtle shifts, recognizing that the cycles change. They are two different ways to look at the Zodiac, and ultimately, they currently vary only slightly.

However, the Earth's equator moves back at about 51" of longitude per year. This is referred to as the "precession of the equinoxes," and it is essential to note: The area Western astronomy refers to as Aries shifts further from the real location that is utilized by the Vedic astrologers by roughly 1 degree per 72 years of time. When you calculate that out, recognizing that the Tropical and Sidereal Aries were together right around 285 AD, you realize that there is a difference in the charts- there is currently roughly 24 degrees apart between them that you must be able to acknowledge. With that knowledge in mind, you can then start to identify where to find the Vedic understanding of the Planets based on adjusting for 24 degrees on a chart. However, at this point in time, that is nearly an entire sign out of alignment.

If you want to continue differentiating the two, you will note that the use of Planet varies as well. In particular, the Vedic astrology chart recognizes only some of the Planets. Uranus and Neptune are left out of Vedic astrology, as is Pluto, which, while no longer a Planet, is still recognized as influential by Western astrology purposes. Despite leaving them out, Vedic astrology also welcomes the sun, the Moon, and Rahu-Ketu—two nodes of the Moon. The Lunar nodes are the points at which the Moon's orbit crosses along the ecliptic, also known as the identified path that the Sun takes around the Earth. Western astrology, while it leaves out the nodes, also includes Uranus, Neptune, and Pluto in calculating the readings. Additionally, it leaves out the constellations that are recognized in Vedic astrology.

Perhaps the largest difference is that Western astrology emphasizes the Sun while the Vedic system focuses more on the Moon. The Sun creates more of a psychological emphasis to define the character of an individual. This is why you see the horoscopes that tell you all about who you are as a person, who to bring into your life, and other similar concepts when utilizing Western astrology. However, Vedic astrology will recognize all aspects of life. The Vedic interpretations are typically far more effective, though they are also complex as well. You will be able to see that Vedic astrology is already more astronomically accurate—it looks at the view of the Planets and how they move. They look at how the Planets move in real-time rather than attempting to sort of generalize and theorize it as you see in Western. This is particularly important because the Sun only changes its placement in the sky and sign once every month or so while the Moon changes every 2.25 days, meaning that your reading will be far more accurate.

Now, this doesn't mean that Western astrology is wrong—it is just different. Western astrology looks at different facts and serves a very different purpose as well. Western astrology is typically marked as more open, but it is ultimately up to you which you prefer and which you choose to emphasize. This book will be primarily focusing on Vedic astrology, so if you are interested in other kinds, you will want to look elsewhere instead.

THE PURPOSE OF VEDIC ASTROLOGY

The purpose of Vedic astrology is to identify the fact that all things in this life are linked. For every action, there is a reaction, and that plays out heavily in Vedic astrology. You can see your karma, your fate, and fortune in the stars. This stems from the Hindu belief of karma and reincarnation—you are a soul that is being reborn. Your life and the suffering that you may go through is already preordained; it is designed based on the karma of your past life.

Karma itself is a bit of a tricky subject—it is something that is tied deeply to your behaviors. Everything that you do in life, ever thought, or behavior creates karma. Karma is what you sow—it is what you put out into the universe, and eventually, you will have to reap it, good or bad. If you do things that are unscrupulous, you may end up creating negative or bad karma that you will have to live with, and that can be a major problem for you in a future life. You will reincarnate—your body may die, but your soul will be reborn in another body in another life at some point in the future. That future life will involve you living out your past lives' karma. The life that you live right now is a direct result of the karma that you have sown in the past.

Now, you may think, then, that you are stuck; that fate is dictated for you. That is not the case. Your situations may be fixed, but you always have a choice. Imagine this: You have grown up poor. Perhaps in a past life, you were bad to people. Now, as retribution, you must live a life in poverty as a child. You have two options here—you can grow up and choose to steal and fall back into those bad habits to try to get by, or you can stop, try to better yourself, and work honestly to create a new life for yourself. Your karma only dictates the world around you and the circumstances of your birth and life. However, you always have a choice.

The reason for this is that the life that you live is only there in the first place to provide lessons that you must learn. The situations that you are in are there to teach your soul a very important lesson that it needs to learn. This is because life is nothing but a vessel for you to learn what you need to be enlightened—you must be able to achieve that understanding that you are one with the universe—that you are one with God around you. Your soul does not exist on its own, and when you let go of those earthly pleasures, you learn to recognize that we are here to learn, and karma dictates what we still have left to discover in our lives.

This is what Vedic astrology taps into—it looks at what your karma looks like. Your soul reincarnates at that place and time for a reason, and that is influential. Vedic astrology begins to understand this. When you stop and look at the birth chart, you are able to start understanding more about what

WHAT IS VEDIC ASTROLOGY | 21

you need to know. It is important that you recognize that you are looking at very real factors and seeing how they influence everything else.

LEARNING TO USE VEDIC ASTROLOGY

Vedic astrology begins with your birth chart—a map of your karma that will show your past, your present, and your future. It shares with you the key to who you are on a deeper level. It will tell you what to expect and how you can begin to understand yourself and all of the readings within it. If you want to use Vedic astrology, the best place to start is learning to understand this birth chart. From there, you can begin to look at other aspects.

Your birth chart wills how you the position of the Planets and constellations at the point of your birth. Calculating this out is far easier than you would think—there are plenty of calculators available to you online that will provide you with your natal chart, allowing you to know exactly what the sky looked like at the place and time of your birth, which will then translate into a birth chart. Your birth chart is a square that is divided up—you will notice that you have four squares that have been rotated onto their points in the center, with eight more triangles around the outside to create one big square. This is important to know—the squares and triangles all represent points that are very important to know to create your own personalized reading.

Step 1: Identifying your rising sign

First, you begin by looking at your rising sign, sometimes referred to as your ascendant. On your chart, this is the square whose corner touches the top of the entire chart. There will be a number there within that point, and that number aligns with a Zodiac sign. 1 translates to Aries, 2 is for Taurus, and so on. We'll be looking at this in more depth later.

VEDIC ASTROLOGY

Step 2: The lords

Next, you identify the lords in your birth chart. This will help to provide information about your life and what you can expect. From the lords of the twelve Houses, you will be able to tell information such as your career, wealth, changes, and more. This is essential to see what your karma has in store for you.

Aspects

From there, you must look at the aspect—this is the influence of other Planets on the Houses based on their own positions. Typically, they will show an aspect of the House opposite to their placement. When they are in aspect, they will change what is happening. It will create a slight alteration to the reading without changing the entire thing.

Conjunctions

Conjunctions are what you will see between Planets based upon how far apart they are on your chart. If you want to be able to understand the conjunctions, you will be looking for Planets that are less than 10 degrees apart. These can be translated in all sorts of ways to influence what is happening in your life as well.

Planetary time periods

Next comes taking a look at Planetary time periods—these are based upon which Planets are controlling your life at that point in time. They are directly related to your understanding of the birth charts that you have seen. If you look at them, you will identify that there are Planets in all of your Houses, and those will influence your life. When your lording Planets are in aspect during major times of your life, you will see that there are all sorts of impacts that they may be reporting.

Interpreting it all

Over time, you discover that there is plenty that you need to understand and implement. It can be difficult at first, but ultimately, you will be able to learn to do it. We'll be going over this in far more depth later in the book, but as you can see, there is plenty that you will need to know if you want to be able to really understand what is going on in your life at any point in time. You must be able to understand and identify the birth chart, the Planets, and how they will influence you over a lifetime.

Remember, just because you are looking at your chart and just because you may see that it says one thing doesn't mean that you are stuck. You can choose to act. You can choose to make a choice that can better yourself. This book will teach you that while the situations that you will experience are fixed, other aspects are not. You can better influence yourself. You can better control your interactions so that you will be successful. Your karma may be set in stone, but everything else can change as you change how you behave. Just because you find yourself in one situation doesn't mean that you are doomed to repeat the same mistakes over and over again. You can change up how you engage with yourself and your fate.

CHAPTER 2:
THE HISTORY OF VEDIC ASTROLOGY

Vedic astrology is ancient—it is believed to go back at least thousands of years. There are recordings of Vedic astrology in the ancient Rig Veda from at least 5000 years ago, though some believe that it may even be from 10,000 BC. No matter what the exact date is, one thing is agreed upon: It is thousands of years old, and those thousands of years do not come lightly. They come with plenty of rich history, learning, spiritual insight, and experiential learning. The modern-day Vedic astrology is recognized as being from Jyotish—the science of light. This is an ancient form of knowledge, and it was, like the Vedas, transmitted via oral memorization.

Eventually, the knowledge related to this astrology became far too complex to simply recite and memorize in oral form. It became necessary at some point along the way to write down the information that was observed. As this happened, Jyotish continually grew more and more codified, meaning that it could also be tracked and transmitted to people without the need for memorization with other people being able to practice it. Eventually, it made its way to the West with the name of Hindu astrology. It eventually became known as Vedic astrology instead. However, that knowledge right there doesn't provide you with very much at all to work on if you are interested in the history—it can be difficult to follow if you don't know where to look.

Within this chapter, we are going to attempt to break down the history into a bit more depth than just that. We will take a look at some of the most influential Vedic texts to provide insight, as well as what is known about the world reach of Vedic astrology, looking at the other cultures that it is believed to have permeated. We will take a look at how it became so traditional in Hindu culture, as well as how it began to catch attention worldwide.

THE ORIGINS OF VEDIC ASTROLOGY

Vedic astrology is believed to have originated from Parasara Muni—the father of Vyasadeva, who recorded the Vedic literature that we know today. Parasara was one of the sages recognized due to the fact that in his treatise that he has written, he records that he learned from both Brahma and Narada, two celestial beings that are recognized regularly in Vedic lore. Though he followed Shiva closer, he also wrote the Vishnu Purana, allowing him to leave his mark with the *Brihat Prasara Hora Sastra*. This is translated as the treatise on time, or the treatise on astrology. This shows us our first glimpse at the natal horoscope—your birth chart, with the twelve Zodiac signs, Houses, nine Planets, and the Lunar Mansions as well. Though not presented in the four Vedas, natal astrology is referenced and related to the timing for sacrificial ceremonies. However, because Parasara recorded this all for us, we know that astrology is there. It has created astrology for an individual's daily lives, and more. Unfortunately, Parasara's is the only remaining Vedic literature with astrology that gives us the full picture of how to use it and what it is

This was one of six disciples that were used to support the rituals that would occur—it was used in its earliest sense in order to identify when sacrificial rituals would occur. It eventually branched out to recognize the Planets, Rahu and Ketu, and everything else that you will see in the book. It was designed to provide a technique to develop individuals, and even today, it is a point of spiritual reference for Hindus around the world.

There are some debates about whether it may be the case that Babylonian astrology influenced the Vedic astrology that we know today, though it is not quite known one way or another. However, we can identify that many of the names in

THE HISTORY OF VEDIC ASTROLOGY | 27

Hindu astrology do identify well with Hellenistic astrology, plus the addition of the Hindu Lunar Mansions. The usage of some Greek terminology relating to Hellenistic astrology shows that there had to have been some sort of influence at some point.

IMPORTANT TEXTS

One of the most pivotal texts that you will see referenced if you look into Vedic astrology deeper is Vedanga Jyotisha. This text is recognized as existing back in 700 BC, though it could have been from even earlier, potentially even from 1400 BC. This text was written to discuss the winter solstice. It was written in both Rigveda and Yajurveda recensions. Because of how it was written, it is likely to be on the earlier side—it is believed that the described solstice happened around 1180 BCE.

The Brahma-Siddhanta, written likely around the 5th century CE, was used to begin to describe how the Planets, sun, and Moon all moved about. It looked at this as a method to manage and record time passage, as well as to create calendars. It provided both math and trigonometry to begin identifying orbits, predictions, and even calculate where the mean positions of different bodies were. It was able to present very large numbers as well. It is important to note that these ancient texts were more in line with astronomy for timekeeping more than beginning to use it as astrology to predict the future as well.

Additionally, you may see the Brihat Samhita. This guide, written in 123 AD by Varahamihira, was designed to discuss just how important Vedic astrology could be. It focused on how public welfare could be benefited and even improved through this process, looking to the stars for answers.

After that, in 470 AD, there were two more texts written. These were the Aryabhateeya and Arya Siddhanta, both of which focused on the math that went into being able to calculate everything out. They looked closely at how astronomical observations were necessary to create accurate Vedic astrology carts, aiding to help make the process even more specific than it once was. This was crucial to success and helped to manage the natal charts that we will be looking at closely in the coming chapters.

VEDIC ASTROLOGY AND THE REST OF THE WORLD

Vedic astrology was not contained just to Hindu cultures—it spread throughout the world and is now seen all over to begin attempting to translate the stars into facts to make sense out of the seemingly-nonsensical world that we live in. It spread from India, where it may very well have been the oldest form of astrology, to the rest of the world to influence others. As a form of astrology that is thousands of years old, there is no way that the knowledge from this source never made its way elsewhere. Let's take a look at some of the ways that this form of astrology managed to spread out and how it interacted with other cultures to develop and evolve to what it is today.

Greece and Vedic astrology

Greece was known as a pioneer of astronomy thanks to the information that they were able to develop over time. It is believed that it was introduced to Vedic astrology in the early centuries of the current era thanks to the presence of *Yavanajataka*, which translates to "Sayings of the Greeks." It was first translated from Greek to Sanskrit by Yavanesvara during that 2nd century CE and was the source of plenty of important information. Between the *Yavanajataka* and the *Aryabhatiya*, there was a 300-year gap, but during that time, it is believed that astronomers were probably preoccupied with attempting to translate the Greek astronomy to Sanskrit. From that point on, there were some changes to Vedic astrology, most notably, the fixing of the Planets in their order, along with information about the Zodiacal signs starting with Aries and the Ascendant. This information, of course, became crucial to the foundation and use of Vedic astrology in the first place.

Westernized Vedic astrology

In the 1980s, Hindu astrology became known as Vedic astrology—it has become quite popular in looking to understand information about the world. It is necessary to learn more about people in general. Remember, Vedic astrology contrasts from Western-style astrology, but that doesn't mean that one is wrong. However, keep in mind that in some Western attempts to understand this form of astrology, you will see them include the outer Planet transits to begin to make predictions as well. Ultimately, there are so many different interpretations that you can make what you will out of it—it is ultimately up to you to figure out how you feel, what you believe, and how you will utilize this information.

CHAPTER 3:
THE VEDIC BIRTH CHART

The most fundamental part of understanding Vedic astrology involves looking at the Vedic birth chart. This birth chart will allow you to see all sorts of information about what you will need to know. If you want to create your own from the moment of your birth, you will need to generate a horoscope online. It will be able to generate what the sky looked at right at the moment of your birth, and you will get something like the image that will follow:

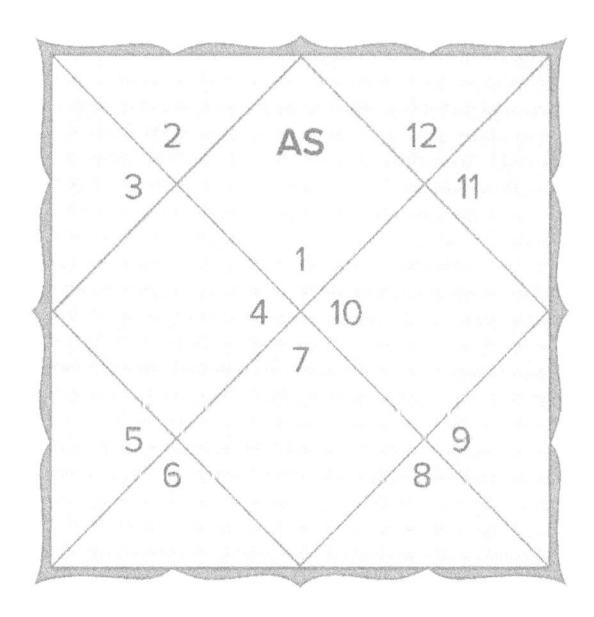

When you look at this image, you can get all sorts of important information from it. You can see that there are 12

different portions that are there for you to understand. Each of the portions is labeled with a number, and those numbers serve as your Houses. Each House is relevant to a different point to consider. When you look at this chart, you get to see all sorts of essential information that will help you.

The chart will tell you just about everything about your life. It will tell you about the information about your personality, your social life, and more. It is there to create that entire map of your life, all by the stars that are available to you at the point of your birth. If you want to better understand your own fate and what there is to understand about yourself, you need to look at this chart.

This chart will show you the positions of all Planets, the Zodiac signs, and constellations. Everything will be contained within this one chart so that you can better understand what you are doing.

As you read throughout this chapter, you will be guided through the general process that you will need to understand. You will learn about the different charts briefly, learning to recognize that there are different forms that you may be introduced to in your endeavors as you work to learn to read Vedic Astrology. Additionally, you will be provided with basic information that will be necessary if you want to be able to better understand the chart that you may have in front of you. You will be guided through identifying the Ascendant on your chart, as well as other pertinent information to what you need to understand. You will see how the Sun and Moon sights matter here as well, and how you can begin to understand them to influence readings. We will also take time to look at the importance of the Planets and what happens with both exaltation and debilitation, two key concepts that you will need a solid understanding of if you want to be successful when it comes to reading charts.

This chapter just barely scratches the surface of information that you need to know—it starts to provide you

THE VEDIC BIRTH CHART | 33

with pertinent information, but there is more to it as well. You will need to continue to read through the book after this chapter to further start to understand the different concepts that you will need to know. Over time, you will achieve a better understanding of the ins and outs of reading the Planets, the stars, and more. Vedic astrology has a large learning curve, but it is worth the effort over time. You will be able to do so much with this information if you are willing to spend the time to read it and commit it to memory.

THE DIFFERENT CHARTS

Now, the chart that you have seen above is the birth chart that you will see throughout the book. This is the North Chart. However, there are several different birth charts that are used in Vedic Astrology. They are dictated by the names of North Indian Chart, South Indian Chart, and East Indian Chart. Each of them is designed slightly differently and works slightly differently, as well. It is important to note that they are all read the same way—you will still have twelve Houses that you look at, and those twelve Houses will be indicative of how you read it. However, they will organize those twelve Houses slightly differently depending upon the version that you are using. No matter how you choose to represent your natal chart, you will still be representing the sky at the moment of your birth in the location of your birth. They will all involve the ascendant and nine Planets in their locations, and they will all yield the same reading.

It ultimately comes down to choosing the chart that you prefer. Throughout the book, we will reference the North Indian Chart, but if you find that you have other preferences, that is fine as well. They are all different box charts—drawn in squares. Let's look over those three different charts now.

North Indian Chart

The North Indian Chart is one in which you will calculate horoscope counter-clockwise from the ascendant. If you look, the Ascendant is at the top, and you can then see a circular pattern that you can rely upon to do your readings effectively. You will notice that each of the twelve Houses will be notable from that center Ascendant. It is typically practiced in areas in Northern India, such as Delhi.

South Indian Chart

The South Indian chart is represented differently. It is calculated with a clockwise pattern instead of counterclockwise from the Ascendant, which can make it somewhat difficult for people who are unfamiliar to use it, but the truth is, it is highly useful and versatile. It can be found to be divided into the same twelve divisions, but they are more or less mirrored. This is typically used in South India, such as Kerala. This chart will have one big square in the center, plus twelve smaller squares along the perimeter, with there being four on each side of the chart. Starting with the one on the top, next to the top left corner, you will go along with numbers, numbering them 1, 2, and so on until you reach the top left corner for number 12. It will still chart everything, but instead of being drawn in squares inside, you will see that you are using that circular clockwise motion.

East Indian Chart

East Indian charts are practiced in Eastern India, as the name implies. It shows those same twelve Houses and divisions, but typically it works a bit differently. It will move counterclockwise, just like the North Indian chart, and is closely related. However, the outside circle is usually lacking.

The Ascendant (*Lagna*)

The Ascendant of the chart is perhaps one of the most important features. It is your sort of guidance that will point out where everything else goes on the chart. This point is different based on the time and place of your birth—every place on Earth will have its own ascendant sign and degree within the 12 Zodiac signs at any point because of the fact that the Planet is always spinning and therefore a different part of the sky will always be visible at that ascendant point. The sky, as it rotates, will always go through all twelve Zodiac signs within a 24 hour period, meaning that every two hours, it will change. Typically, we are able to point to the rising sign at the time of birth as being the true one indicative of emotional and spiritual attributes that we possess.

This is one of the most significant readings that you will have on your chart. It is believed to provide all sorts of information about you to determine what you are and who you will become as an adult. That Ascendant becomes necessary for you to understand and recognize. It is the condition of the sky at the point of introduction to the world, and it will show how you tend to approach everything around you as a result. Let's look at some of the most significant points that your Ascendant will reveal for you:

How you appear as a person, physically and mentally—you will be able to point to your Ascendant as highly influential over your physical form as well as your personality.

- Your physical stature—your body is influenced by the stars in the sky as well.

- Information about your health and how you will do in life. Physical fitness aside, some people are simply healthier, while others tend to be sicker. This is related to the Ascendant.

- The struggles that you will face in life, as well as the achievements and endeavors that you will pursue in your life as well. It is highly indicative of how you are able to approach the situation and what you may choose to do with yourself.

- Your fortune throughout life, including your general circumstances that you were born into (i.e., if you were born into poverty or wealth).

- The degree to which you will discover that the circumstances of your birth will influence the rest of your life, determining whether you are going to be caught up in repeating mistakes of the past or if you will be able to succeed despite any sort of struggles that you may face.

- The story of the individual's life and how it will relate to what will happen in the future—you can identify if someone will travel abroad or succeed somewhere further away.

- Information about relationships with siblings and more.

The point of birth is typically alongside the specific degree of your Ascendant at that point of birth. That degree is necessary to better understand just how significantly your Ascendant will be able to influence you. It determines whether you are highly influenced by it or if you may be under more of an influence of others. People with lower degrees of Ascendant will usually be impacted less by their Ascendant than those who have higher degrees. In the next chapter, as we go over the different Zodiacal signs, we will be discussing what it means to be ascendant in each of these different signs so that you can begin to better understand how someone is going to be influenced.

The ascendant point is the point to the true east of a place and is the space and time signature of the individual. It will also show up as the first House on your chart—it will be in the point labeled as 1 AS on the chart that was provided earlier in this chapter. That sign then continues throughout the other charts as well. If the First House is Aries, for example, meaning that your Ascendant sign was Aries, then Taurus is in the second House. This will continue throughout all of the different Houses, creating a chart in which each of the 12 Zodiac has a place and a role in your life.

THE VEDIC BIRTH CHART| 37

In future chapters, we will be looking more at how the Ascendant is able to influence so much about you, especially when you then compare it to other points as well. However, for now, be aware that your Ascendant will become highly important to you—you will need this sign so that you can be certain that you are on the right track.

This natal chart, the birth chart, shows the exact signs and star alignment at the moment of your birth and is permanent—it will always look exactly as it is at that point and you'll be able to read that to get plenty of information to translate into the reading for life.

FINDING THE POSITION OF THE SUN AND MOON

After you've got your Ascendant, the rest of your birth chart is able to be interpreted well—you know the placement of all of the signs in the different Houses and that means that you can then begin to apply the Planetary locations as well to be certain that you know where everything out to go. This is where you start to look at the positions of everything else.

The Sun and Moon aspects show us some very significant information on our birth chart—they recognize the duality of our conscious wants and unconscious needs. They are literally night and day, and they show plenty of information between them. The relationship between these two celestial bodies shows plenty of information about ourselves as well as our parental figures. Those that are in conjunct, flowing well, tend to create positive impacts upon our lives, creating positivity. However, if negative, there may be plenty of struggling with trying to figure out what is right.

You will have Sun and Moon signs that will help you to understand the life that you've got as well. Thankfully, rather than having to calculate this out for yourself, there are plenty of calculators that you can use to figure out the exact positions of the Sun and Moon at the moment of your birth. Your Sun and Moon signs can have very different impacts upon you. Let's look at these in a bit more depth now.

Moon sign

Your Moon sign will provide you with plenty of information that becomes critical to understand if you want to be able to better understand your own personality. Let's go over some of the key elements that you can expect to see by looking to your Moon sign:

Your character, personality, preferences, behavioral patterns, and nature, along with any inherent tendencies or attributes

- The current path of your fate so that you can drive yourself in the right direction.

- A role in your ability to find compatibility with your future spouse, as well as your other friends and family members.

- Identifying the luck and harmony in your relationships that you have

- Mental compatibility with others based upon their own personal Moon signs

- Day to day predictions and scenarios based upon your Moon sign

Your Moon sign, just as your others, will be influenced by your Zodiac. Each of the twelve Zodiac will create a different sort of effect when the Moon is in them. Let's go over the meanings of those briefly now:

- **Aries:** You are likely to be impatient in life, as well as impulsive, but you will be quite skilled and active in the pursuit of knowledge.

- **Taurus:** This is a favorable placement—when the Moon sign is Taurus, the individual will be quite stable mentally.

- **Gemini:** You may struggle with duality of the mind—everything will be hot and cold or good and bad. You will struggle to find that middle ground.

- **Cancer:** You are likely to be kind to all around you, taking care of the people in your life, and working to be the "mother" of your group, no matter where you go.

- **Leo:** You are a natural-born leader and are likely strong and willing to exert authority

- **Virgo:** You will most likely be very practical in everything that you do approach around you.

- **Libra:** Your mind will remain balanced, but you will find that you also must constantly be balancing things in order to be able to make good progress.

- **Scorpio:** This is an unfavorable position for the Moon—there are plenty of fluctuations and struggles when your Moon sign is Scorpio. You may find that your mind is constantly changing.

- **Sagittarius:** You are likely to be very religiously oriented.

- **Capricorn:** You are likely to be highly stable with your ability to make thoughts and judgments while also making it a point to remain rigid.

- **Aquarius:** You are likely to be someone open to communication and social interaction. You will likely find that you constantly desire to be part of lots of different groups as much as possible.

- **Pisces:** You are likely to orient yourself toward spiritual aspects in your life, and you will focus elsewhere other than home.

As you can see, the Moon sign can play a role in just about every aspect of your life, and you will need to be mindful of this. You must make sure that you work hard to regulate your understanding of the Moon sign.

Sun sign

Vedic astrology emphasizes the importance of the Moon sign, but the Sun sign can also be influential. It is able to show off some of your innermost characteristics based upon the position of the Sun at any point in time. Keep in mind that while the Moon changes signs regularly, the Sun remains in any sign for upwards of a month at a time. Let's go over the basic readings for these now:

- **Aries:** *April 14 to May 14*—This person is likely to be highly idealistic and focused on leading well. They are typically compassionate and intelligent

- **Taurus:** *May 15 to June 14*—This person is likely to value tradition and family above all else, focusing on remaining distinguished

- **Gemini:** *June 15 to July 17*— This person is likely to be highly compassionate, willing to value their friendship to maintain an amicable relationship with others, and working together in groups. Typically they are inclusive and intelligent.

- **Cancer:** *July 18 to August 15*—This person is likely to have a high work ethic and constantly focus on achieving goals. They are usually quite authoritative and will do whatever it takes to maintain their values at the end of the day.

THE VEDIC BIRTH CHART | 41

- **Leo:** *August 17 to September 16*—This person will be highly intellectual and capable of restraint, though they will also be highly comfortable with their power and playing politics. They may even err on the side of manipulative

- **Virgo:** *September 17 to October 17*—This person is highly driven toward perfection and attempting to find a way to manage service. They may be somewhat controlling at times.

- **Libra:** *October 18 to November 16*—This person is likely to be highly influential and successful in business.

- **Scorpio:** *November 17 to December 15* -- This person is likely to be highly influenced by knowledge, able to research well, and heal. They usually find that they are willing to love others as well.

- **Sagittarius:** *December 16 to Jan 15*-- When the Sun is in this sign, you will see that the individual is highly religious and engaging in spiritual matters. Typically, they will take a highly liberal attitude

- **Capricorn:** *January 16 to February 12*— These people are typically highly influenced by their goals—they will pursue them, and they want to live a good comfortable life with good karma

- **Aquarius:** *February 13 to March 12*—These people are highly intelligent and creative. They are usually skilled and able to perfect their karma as well. They tend to err on the side of diplomatic and engaging, though they may sometimes be good with their hands and tools.

- **Pisces:** *March 15 to April 13*— These people are typically calm and intelligent. They tend to align well with being creative, dreaming, being risk-takers, and creating. However, they may also be deceptive

FINDING THE PLANETS' POSITIONS

Each Planet on your chart will influence the way that you behave as an individual. We are physical and spiritual at the same time, and because of this, our bodies are able to be altered. We are connected to the universe, and in that connection, we are a part of the endless cycle, which is highly influenced by the universe around us. Because of this, we look to the positions of the Planets. They have their effect because we are just as much of a part of the universe as they are—they influence us based upon their exact positions at the moment of our birth. The forces of the universe are able to alter our thoughts, which also influence our feelings as a direct result. We become people that are driven by these physical heavenly bodies, the luminaries, and Rahu and Ketu.

Finding their positions can be somewhat difficult if you don't yet know what you are doing—it can be tough to figure out where they were at that exact moment of your birth, but thankfully, there is no shortage of calculators that will do the work for you. Online, you can simply put in the date of your birth, the time, and your location of birth so that you will be able to calculate out the array of the Planets onto your own chart

When you have the positions down, you will be able to begin interpreting them. In the coming chapters, you will first get to know the significance of each of the Planets and their meanings. Additionally, when we look at the different Houses, we will look at what happens when each Planet is in each House, looking at the meanings that they have and how they may influence the life that you will have. Being able to do this, to look at the differences between the Planets, the Houses, and the signs will help you to learn everything that you need to know to begin interpreting those charts and figuring out what you want to do.

THE VEDIC BIRTH CHART | 43

SIGNIFICATORS *(KARKA)*

Another point to consider when reading your chart is to look at significators. Each House will have its own significators. These are the purposes of those particular Houses—it means that when you look at that particular House, you are always looking at a reading for that particular Planet. After you have placed your Planets on your chart, you are able to start interpreting them to figure out what is meant by each of them. Now, we will be addressing the Houses in depth in Chapter 6, but you do need to know about this concept, as we will be addressing them as well when you look at the Planets. Each Planet, like the Houses, will have their own significator—they all get meanings that are directly related to them. The Moon, for example, will always represent the mind and emotion. Additionally, the First House will always be the Ascendant. As you read through your chart, you will be able to see the different significator, and when they are able to align just right, you will get different impacts. We will be getting into this all throughout the rest of the book as well, at which point you will be able to put more context together to better understand the concept.

EXALTATION AND DEBILITATION

You will also have to consider the exaltation and debilitation of the Planets in your chart as well. Planets have specific areas where they work well, where they are comfortable and able to truly shine with their influence over you. However, there are also periods of time where they are not able to do so—where they struggle. You will see this listed in the lists of information that you will be dealing with in the next chapter—you will see that there are both exaltation and debilitation points that are listed. This means that when the Planets are in those different positions on your chart with those particular signs, you will start to see different effects that will change up how your own fate plays out

Exaltation

First, let's address exaltation. This is that location on your chart where the Planets thrive—it is that space in which they will be able to better influence everything else around them. The Exaltation points in your life are there for a reason—they are there to show that your Planets are particularly influential over you. They are necessary so that you can predict how well you will do in your life.

Planets that are exalted in your chart are those that will show you that you are strong. They will represent the happiness that you can expect to see in your life. They are special influencers that will help the greatest. Let's take a look at the different Planets and see where they are best exalted:

- **Sun (*Aries 10 degrees*):** When exalted, the Sun will give your overall status and happiness. Your relationship with your father will be influenced here

- **Moon (*Taurus 3 degrees*):** When in exaltation, you can see that you will be famous and enjoy the success in your career. You will also find that your relationship with your mother is influenced here.

- **Mars (*Capricorn 28 degrees*):** This exaltation will create happiness and prosperity—you will find that you are content in your possessions and your land. You will also find that you are supported well by your brothers and that you have a comfortable status in life.

- **Mercury (*Virgo 15 degrees*):** When Mercury is in exaltation, you will realize that you are highly intelligent. You will have a great immune system and recovery, and you will usually be highly knowledgeable.

- **Jupiter (*Cancer 5 degrees*):** This exaltation implies that you will be highly influential of the knowledge that you get to experience, and finances will flow as a result.

THE VEDIC BIRTH CHART | 45

- **Venus (*Pisces 27 degrees*)**: This exaltation is related to luxury, romance, and fun. It is closely related to your relationship with your spouse.

- **Saturn (*Libra 20 degrees*)**: When Saturn is exalted, you will have great luck in career and status.

Debilitation

On the other hand, the debilitation is the exact opposite. Debilitation is the point in your chart in which the Planets will work unfavorably. If you are suffering negatively in your life, it could be that you are struggling due to your debilitation. This happens when the Planet is placed in an area where it struggles—it is unable to be strong or powerful because of its location and proximity to its debilitating constellation, and as a result, they struggle. Now, let's look over this point as well to better understand what will happen as you continue to struggle in your life:

- **Sun (*Libra 10 degrees*)**: When in debilitation, you want to avoid legal matters. You and your relationship with the government should be avoided.

- **Moon (*Scorpio 3 degrees*)**: You may find that your mindset rapidly and regularly changes at a whim, and you realize that you are stuck. The Moon is a great barrier to your happiness.

- **Mars (*Cancer 28 degrees*)**: During the debilitation of Mars, you will struggle with property and likely argue with siblings

- **Mercury (*Pisces 15 degrees*)**: With the debilitation of Mercury, you will find that you struggle with your sister or sisters, and you may struggle with math.

- **Jupiter (*Capricorn 5 degrees*)**: When you have Jupiter being debilitated, you usually end up in a position where your finances are set back significantly for some reason or another.

- **Venus *(Virgo 27 degrees)*:** When in debilitation, you will realize that Venus cause struggles in romantic endeavors and contexts. You will struggle in your married life, and you will likely lack love in that relationship.

- **Saturn *(Aries 20 degrees)*:** When in debilitation, you will realize that you will struggle in your career and relationship. Saturn in debilitation is not a kind placement at all.

CHAPTER 4:
THE PLANETS (*GRAHAS*)

Now, the defining feature of astrology is the Planets—we know this. We look at more than just the Sun when understanding at Vedic astrology. We know that the Sun is important, and we will address its value shortly, but there is more to it than just that. The Sun is important alongside the other bodies in the sky.

Depending upon the placement and relation to each other, the Planets can have all sorts of different meanings. For different people, those same bodies can mean very different things based upon one's birth chart. This is precisely why so many people can have different experiences despite the fact that all of the Planets are the same for all of us. It's not like Venus is suddenly in a different spot for one person, and the next when two people have different experiences—their birth chart is what varies from person to person. The birth chart of one person may dictate that their Tenth House is Venus while the other may have Venus in the second House. This means that the pattern may be entirely different people.

Of course, the Planets will still have very similar meanings—they will be related to similar aspects in life, but they will align into different Houses for different people. Within this chapter, we will be looking to understand the Planets and their meanings so that we can see what they mean in your own birth charts. They all have their own important meanings that you will have to acknowledge, and that is something that must be understood bare minimum. As you read through this chapter, you will learn what each of the Planets represents as well as the information about the sun, the Moon, and the nodes of the Moon. We will also be taking some time to understand the conditions of the Planets as well so that you can see how they interact with each other. This information all becomes crucial if you want to be able to understand the Planets and how they work in relation to Vedic astrology.

UNDERSTANDING THE PLANETS AND THEIR POSITIONS

First, it is important to understand that in Vedic astrology, Planets are listed as both benefics and malefics. This will help you important to understand the rules that these Planets have so that you can better recognize that they have their own personal meanings. When you want to be able to recognize what they do and how they interact, you will be able to do this through looking at the Planets that are deemed benefics or malefics and where they are placed.

This is yet another place where you will see the difference between Western and Vedic astrology play out. In Western astrology, you will note that there is good and bad in every Planet, though Vedic astrology likes to refer to certain Planets as beneficial while the others are difficult to deal with. In

The benefic Planets and Houses

As the name implies, benefic Planets are *beneficial*. They are good Planets that are meant to be seen as generally good for you and the situation. Several Planets are recognized as benefic. These include Mercury, the Moon, Venus, and Jupiter. Additionally, certain Houses are believed to be benefic as well. The favorable Houses are those of 1, 2, 4, 5, 7, 9, and 10. Planets that fall into these Houses are typically seen as favorable.

The malefic Planets

On the other hand, there are several Planets and Houses that would be referred to as malefic. These are bad or malevolent

THE PLANETS (GRAHAS) | 49

Houses if you need a way to remember them. The malefic Planets include the Sun, Mars, Rahu and Ketu, and Saturn. Additionally, you will see that Houses 6, 8, and 12 are considered malefic as well.

Neutral Houses

After dividing the Houses into both malefic and benefic, you will note that there are two that are missing. These are 3 and 11, and they are typically considered neutral depending upon the rulers at that point in time.

THE SUN (RAVI OR SURYA)

Gender: *Masculine*

Significator: *The soul*

Relationship: The father

Planetary Cabinet: King

Temperament: Fixed and steady

Element: Fire

Quality: Serenity

Caste: Warrior

Nature: Malefic

Strength: Tenth House

Weakness: Fourth House

Zodiacal Sign: Leo

Zodiacal House: Fifth

Exaltation: Aries

Debilitation: Libra

Determent: Aquarius

Friends: Moon, Jupiter, Mars

Neutral: Mercury

Enemies: Venus and Saturn

Vimshottari Dasha: Six Years

Lunar Mansions: Krittika, Uttara Ashadha, Uttara Phalguni

THE PLANETS (GRAHAS) | 51

The first celestial body that we will address is not technically a Planet, but it falls into one of the spots nonetheless. The Sun is responsible for our physical health. It is necessary to rule over our sense of ego and how we project ourselves into the world around us. It is the closest star to us, and it is responsible for the light that we have. As it is central to the solar system, it never enters retrograde thanks to the fact that it is stationary. In Hindu mythology, the Sun God is the source of energy and life within the world.

It will provide control over your life force—the prana within you. Based on the placement of the sun, you will have different functionality in the body. In particular, it is responsible for controlling the heart, eyes, back, and circulation, and when you see that you suffer from heart problems, typically, it has to do with the Sun and its placement in your horoscope.

In terms of ruled professions, the Sun controls those that have power. It is highly linked to high-ranking government roles, as well as employment in wool, gold, wood, and similar fields. It can also be linked to jobs that are in entertainment or involving children.

If you find that the Sun is in a malefic House, there are some things that you can do to help—you can try any of the following:

Worship Lord Shiva, the deity of the Sun

- Reciting Sun mantras
- Fast on Sundays
- Wear one or twelve Mukhi Rudraksh
- Perform the Surya Namaskar
- Donate wheat on Sundays

THE MOON (*CHANDRA*)

Gender: *Feminine*

Significator: *Emotion and the mind*

Relationship: *Mother*

Planetary Cabinet: *Queen*

Temperament: *Changeable and Fickle*

Element: *Water*

Quality: *Serenity*

Caste: *Trader*

Nature: *Benefic and Malefic*

Strength: *Fourth House*

Weakness: *Tenth House*

Zodiacal Sign: *Cancer*

Zodiacal House: *Fourth House*

Exaltation: *Taurus*

Debilitation: *Scorpio*

Determent: *Capricorn*

Friends: *Mercury and Sun*

Neutral: *Saturn, Jupiter, Mars, Venus*

Enemies: *None*

Vimshottari Dasha: *Ten years*

Lunar Mansions: *Rohini Nakshatra, Hasta Nakshatra, Shravana Nakshatra*

THE PLANETS (GRAHAS) | 53

Like the sun, the Moon is not defined as a Planet in astronomy, but in astrology, it fits the bill. It is highly influential as it circles around the Earth and is one of the most defining bodies in Vedic astrology in the first place. In Hindu mythology, the Moon was worshipped by all celestials. He had twenty-seven wives, all sisters, and daughters of Daksha. He preferred just one, Rohini, but the other twenty-six were not satisfied. They asked him to spend time with them as well. They then moved on to speak to their father, who attempted to reason with the Moon but was ignored. The Moon was then cursed to suffer from consumption.

Every day, the Moon faded away, losing his glow. Due to the concern for Earth, Daksha was asked to change the curse—he modified it to cause the Moon to wane for fourteen days, then gain back his form for fourteen days, but he had to spend one day with each wife. This created the waxing and waning of the Moon that we know today.

In Vedic astrology, the Moon is believed to control all sorts of parts of the body. In particular, it maintains power over the breasts, ribs, womb, stomach, alimentary canal, and the cycle of menstruation. It is able to influence the body greatly in these areas and therefore is important to recognize.

The Moon is able to influence our emotions and how we feel mentally. When it is placed well on a chart, it tends to create and influence happiness, attractiveness, and accomplishments. However, when the Moon is in a bad House, it tends to be a problem—it can lead to anxiety and hardship, or even depression.

This body is able to rule over careers in fluid-related fields, such as farming milk, fishing, and brewers. Similarly, it also controls real estate, public relations, and more. It is greatly related to manufacturing, farming, sugar, and restaurants as well.

If you find that your Moon is not placed well, there are things that you can do to try to assuage this. These include:

- Worshipping the deity of the Moon
- Reciting Moon mantras
- Donating milk, rice, and cloth on Mondays to virgin women
- Fasting on Mondays
- Wear two Mukhi Rudraksh

MERCURY (BUDHA)

Gender: Neutral

Significator: Speech

Relationship: Maternal uncles

Planetary Cabinet: Crown prince

Temperament: Versatile and volatile

Element: Earth

Quality: Passionate and imperious

Caste: Trader

Nature: Benefic with benefic Planets, but it can be malefic

Strength: First House

Weakness: Seventh House

Zodiacal Sign: Gemini and Virgo

Zodiacal House: Third and Sixth Houses

Exaltation: Virgo

Debilitation: Pisces

Determent: Sagittarius

Friends: Sun and Venus

Neutral: Moon and Mars

Enemies: Jupiter and Saturn

Vimshottari Dasha: Seventeen years

Lunar Mansions: Revati Nakshatra, Alesha Nakshatra, Jyestha Nakshatr

Mercury is the quickest Planet in the solar system and is closely related to intelligence and communication. When you've got a strong Mercury, you usually are highly intelligent and highly dexterous thanks to the ruling over the hands. You will likely find that communication is easy if you've got a strong Mercury as well.

In Hindu mythology, Mercury is the son of the Moon. Moon was able to conquer three different worlds and completed the Rajsu yagna, which provided him lordship. He ruled over many, and over time, he grew arrogant. He eloped with Jupiter's wife, Tara, and refused to return her. A war broke out and lasted for so long that Brahma asked the Moon to return Tara. The Moon complied, but she returned pregnant. Upon returning, Jupiter demanded that she abort the child, and the baby survived. The child glowed gold, and Jupiter claimed paternity of the child. However, Moon also claimed paternity, and Brahma had to question her to get the answer—she admitted that Moon had fathered the child, who we know now as Mercury.

In terms of the body, it is able to rule the nervous system, which is where it gets its power over mental wellness. It is commonly related to the nervousness and tension that people feel. It is the messenger of the nervous system, much like it is the messenger to the gods, and it is able to send those nerve impulses throughout the body. It is also responsible for hormones and digestive systems as well.

This Planet is able to influence all sorts of professions as well. In particular, it focuses on those surrounding knowledge and communication, as well as travel. This brings it around to also ruling over trade and similar professions. If it requires communication, strong memory, and travel, it is likely to be governed by Mercury. This puts it in control of advertising, auditors, math, teachers, journalists, and more.

If you want to fix a problem due to placement, the best thing that you can do is work to worship the deity of

Mercury—Lord Vishnu. You can also recite Mercury mantras, or donate green beans to Eunuchs on Wednesdays. Fasting should also happen on Wednesdays, and you can wear four Mukhi Rudraksh.

VENUS (SHUKRA)

Gender: Feminine

Significator: Desire and Potency

Relationship: Spouse

Planetary Cabinet: Royal Advisor

Temperament: Accommodating and Easygoing

Element: Water

Quality: Passionate and Imperious

Caste: Priest

Nature: Benefic

Strength: Fourth House

Weakness: Tenth House

Zodiacal Sign: Libra and Taurus

Zodiacal House: Saturn and Mercury

Exaltation: Pisces

Debilitation: Virgo

Determent: Aries

Friends: Mercury and Saturn

Neutral: Mars and Jupiter

Enemies: Moon and Sun

Vimshottari Dasha: Twenty years

Lunar Mansions: Purva Ashadha Nakshatra, Purva Phalguny Nakshatra, Bharani Nakshatra

This Planet is the Planet of love, representing the feminine and beauty, along with all kinds of pleasures. A strong Venus creates artistic appreciation and strong, lasting marriages. When Venus is weak, on the other hand, it leads to problems with relationships in the future.

In Hindu mythology, Venus is able to raise the dead that has fallen in battles with gods. He is smart and skilled in learning all kinds of knowledge. He is strong, handsome, and just as sensuous as he is skilled. He is highly virile and is the son of Rishi Bhrigu, borne of his father Brahma's semen.

This Planet presides over Taurus and Libra, and with them is able to regulate the throat, the kidneys, and the thyroid, along with several vitamins and minerals. He controls the veins of the body along with the skin. Venus is typically to blame when there is a problem with the blood and the ability to relax the muscles. Throat problems and thyroid problems, along with diabetes, tend to be related to Venus.

In terms of professions that are ruled by Venus, you would see all things related to art and beauty, along with anything luxurious. It is capable of influencing taxes, finances, sweets, oils, tobacco, and more, along with many of the acting careers, such as music, painting, drawing, sculpting, photography, jewelry, and more.

When Venus is not in a good spot on the horoscope, you have other actions that you can take, such as worshipping the goddess Shakti or Durga. You could also recite the Venus mantras. If looking to charity to aid in the placement of Venus, you could donate perfumes to married women on Fridays, or you could choose to fast on Friday as well.

MARS (KUJA OR MANGAL)

Gender: *Masculine*

Significator: *Power and strength*

Relationship: *Siblings*

Planetary Cabinet: *Army commander*

Temperament: *Rash, angry, and violent*

Element: *Fire*

Quality: *Ignorant or dull*

Caste: *Warrior*

Nature: *Malefic*

Strength: *Tenth House*

Weakness: *Fourth House*

Zodiacal Sign: *Aries and Scorpio*

Zodiacal House: *First and Eighth Houses*

Exaltation: *Capricorn*

Debilitation: *Cancer*

Determent: *Libra*

Friends: *Moon, Sun, and Jupiter*

Neutral: *Saturn and Venus*

Enemies: *Mercury*

Vimshottari Dasha: *Seven Years*

Lunar Mansions: *Chitra, Mrigashira, Dhanishta*

THE PLANETS (GRAHAS) | 61

Mars is the Planet of athletes and action. It is able to show power and initiative as well. Those with a strong Mars tend to be willing to work harder, show that they are able to make changes, and find that they are able to withstand keeping up with their effort. However, those with afflicted Mars may show that they fight too much or find that they are heavily punished.

In Hindu mythology, Daksha, the king of Earth, invited all of the gods and demigods to the greatest yagna—a sacrifice. However, he did not invite his son in law, Lord Shiva. Lord Shiva's wife went to go anyway, but when she arrived, her father insulted her husband. Hurt by his words, she gave up her life. Lord Shiva, upon hearing what had happened, he pulled a hair out of his head and threw it on the ground. It became a being with great power and a fearsome look. Lord Shiva named him Virabhadra and told him that he had to destroy Daksha and his yagna. Virabhadra did so, destroying the sacrifice, and killed Daksha. Upon his return, he was granted a place in the heavens as Mars.

In terms of the body that is ruled by this particular Planet, you can see that physical and mental energy are both highly influenced by it. It is able to control our reproductive organs along with the muscular system, blood, and more. Anemia tends to be directly related to this Planet as well, along with any types of inflammation and fever that may be suffered. When well-placed, however, sickness is not as much of a concern.

When it comes to the professions that are ruled by this Planet, you will see those such as people in violent, volatile, or unpredictable situations. This includes the army, police officers, firefighters, those responsible for weapons and artillery, or contact sports. Additionally, those careers such as surgeons and butchers are also related to this particular Planet.

If you have to deal with a poorly placed Mars in your horoscope, there are ways for you to cope. Some of the best ways to do so include worshipping the deity of Mars, or through reciting Mars mantras. Additionally, you can donate red cloth on Tuesdays to young males, or fasting on Tuesdays. You can also wear three Mukhi Rudraksh.

JUPITER (GURU OR BRIHASPATI)

Gender: Masculine

Significator: Fortune and knowledge

Relationship: Children

Planetary Cabinet: royal advisor

Temperament: Soft-hearted, benign, and mild

Element: Ether

Quality: Serenity

Caste: Priest

Nature: Benefic

Strength: First House

Weakness: Seventh House

Zodiacal Sign: Sagittarius and Pisces

Zodiacal House: Ninth and Twelfth House

Exaltation: Cancer

Debilitation: Capricorn

Determent: Gemini

Friends: Mars, Moon, Sun

Neutral: Saturn

Enemies: Venus and Mercury

Vimshottari Dasha: sixteen years

Lunar Mansions: Purva Bhadra Nakshatra, Vishakha Nakshatra, Punarvasu Nakshatra

Jupiter is deemed the Great Benefic, representing religion and wisdom, as well as expansion and growth. Wealth is also ruled by Jupiter. Those who have Jupiter in their favor will typically be adherent to religions, usually their parents. Typically, they are also wealthy and well-educated. On the other hand, those with Jupiter in unfavorable positions find that they are unable to enjoy prosperity or religious happiness.

In Hindu mythology, Jupiter was one of the eight sons of Angiras, son of Brahma. He received knowledge from his father and then left in hopes of identifying spiritual knowledge. He spent thousands of years meditating, and in return, he was able to earn a position as Guru to the demigods. He had the job of guiding the gods and demigods.

In terms of the body, Jupiter is related to physical growth and expansion. It shows swelling and abnormal expansion. This includes liver and other diseases related to it. You can also see Jupiter related to the fats in the body and how they are broken down.

In terms of the professions that Jupiter governs, you can expect them to be highly related to spirituality, the law, wealth, religion, and other such jobs. People who are in holy places also are ruled by Jupiter as well. It is related to religion, faith, and spiritualism. Additionally, you can expect to see agents and brokers ruled by Jupiter.

If you find that Jupiter is in an unfavorable position, you want to consider actions such as worshipping Lord Shiva, the ruling deity. Additionally, you can recite Jupiter mantras, Donating bananas, yellow clothes, and saffron or turmeric to priests on Thursdays. Additionally, you can expect to see fasting on Thursdays, helping you as well.

SATURN (*SHANI*)

Gender: Gender-neutral

Significator: Misfortune and Grief

Relationship: Subordinates

Planetary Cabinet: Servant

Temperament: Harsh, insensitive, and cruel

Element: Air

Quality: Dull or ignorant

Caste: Lower caste

Nature: Malefic

Strength: Seventh House

Weakness: First House

Zodiacal Sign: Aquarius and Capricorn

Zodiacal House: Tenth and Eleventh

Exaltation: Libra

Debilitation: Aries

Determent: Leo

Friends: Venus and Mercury

Neutral: Jupiter

Enemies: Mars, Moon, and Sun

Vimshottari Dasha: Nineteen Years

Lunar Mansions: Uttara Bhadra Nakshatra, Anuradha Nakshatra, Pushya Nakshatra

Saturn is responsible for the skeletal system along with teeth and skin. Additionally, you can see that rheumatism and arthritis are highly related to Saturn. Saturn, ruling over Aquarius and Capricorn, along with all diseases. Additionally, you can see that knees and the legs are highly related to Saturn, as well as the spinal cord and muscles, nerves, and brain. This means that multiple sclerosis is also closely related.

Saturn is also responsible for careers that are difficult or traditional as well. These are jobs that are responsible for domestic work, factories, servants, labor and manual work, and more. Additionally, you can expect to see that priests and monks are closely related to Saturn thanks to strict rules and conservative and lonely lives. It is also associated with theft, plundering, or other criminal activity.

If you find that your Saturn is in the wrong position, you can find relief in all sorts of ways, such as worshipping Lord Hanuman, reciting Saturn mantras, donating black cloths, and iron on Saturdays to old men, fasting on Saturdays or wearing seven Mukhi Rudraksh.

RAHU (NODE OF THE MOON)

Gender: *Feminine*

Significator: *Spiritual knowledge*

Relationship: *Maternal grandparents*

Planetary Cabinet: *None*

Temperament: *Unpredictable*

Element: *Air*

Quality: *Ignorant and Dull*

Caste: *Outcast-- none*

Nature: *Malefic*

Strength: *None*

Weakness: *None*

Zodiacal Sign: None

Zodiacal House: None

Exaltation: *Taurus*

Debilitation: *Scorpio*

Determent: *None*

Friends: *Venus, Mars, and Saturn*

Neutral: *Jupiter and Mercury*

Enemies: Moon *and Sun*

Vimshottari Dasha: *Eighteen Years*

Lunar Mansions: *Ardra Nakshatra, Shatabhisha Nakshatra, Swati Nakshatra*

Rahu is the north Lunar node—it is the point at which the upper orbital path of the Moon meets the orbital path of the sun. It is typically deemed a malefic, but when well-placed, it can also be a point of success. Typically, when afflicted, it causes problems based upon the connected Planets. These typically involve problems with boundaries.

In Hindu mythology, the Rahu is the son of Viprachitti and Simhika. Rahu is the head which has been dismembered from the body or Ketu. The legend goes that the demigods were losing power due to a curse, and because of that, they appealed to Lord Brahma. As a result, Brahma guided them to Lord Vishnu, and together, they planned to ask the Asuras for the nectar of immortality, which the demigods could share with the Asuras. The Asuras agreed, acknowledging that they would need to work together, so off they went. They managed to get the nectar, and the Asuras chose to keep it for themselves. Lord Vishnu had to get it back and incarnated as a beautiful enchantress. They agreed to give her the nectar. Rahu chose to hide as a demigod and sat between the Sun and Moon gods. They told Vishnu who he was, and Vishnu severed his head. However, because he had already gotten a drop of nectar, he was immortal. They then became separate entities thanks to the nectar, and both constantly chase after the Sun and Moon in order to get revenge.

Rahu does not rule over any body parts, but it can influence those that t is in conjunction or aspect with. It is able to, however, govern epidemics, insanity, and poisoning. Rahu has similar impacts on people as Saturn. Additionally, it is able to relate to the arts and magic.

When Rahu is not in alignment, one of the best things that you can do is work on worshiping Lord Shiva, reciting the Rahu mantras, donating blue clothes, or coconut to beggars on Saturdays. Additionally, fasting on Saturdays and wearing eight Mukhi Rudraksh.

KETU (NODE OF THE MOON)

Gender: *Neutral*

Significator: *Final liberation*

Relationship: *Paternal parents*

Planetary Cabinet: *None*

Temperament: *Unpredictable*

Element*: Fire*

Quality: *Ignorant*

Caste*: None*

Nature: *Malefic*

Strength: *None*

Weakness: *None*

Zodiacal Sign: *None*

Zodiacal House: *None*

Exaltation: *Scorpio*

Debilitation: *Taurus*

Determent: *None*

Friends: *Venus, Mars, Saturn*

Neutral: *Mercury and Jupiter*

***Enemies: Moon** and Sun*

Vimshottari Dasha: *Seven years*

Lunar Mansions: *Ashwini Nakshatra, Magha Nakshatra, Mula Nakshatra*

Ketu is Rahu's headless body. It is the other Moon's node. It is responsible for the same parts of the body and life as Rahu. Ketu, the South Node, is related to the Dragons Tail and is responsible for technical trades. If your Ketu is in a bad placement, you can fix this through worshipping Lord Ganesha, reciting Keto mantras, donating brown cloths, to beggars, or feed black dogs on Thursdays. Additionally, fasting on Thursdays or wearing nine Mukhi Rudraksh.

PLANETARY CONDITIONS

Planets have five conditions that they can have. They have five distinct relationships that can be had by combining two other types as well. There are permanent relationships, and there are temporary relationships. Permanent relationships are, as the name implies, permanent. They don't change. The position of the Planets does not change up how they interact with each other. No matter where they fall on a birth chart, they can always have these same relationships. These are what we identified when you had the friends, enemies, and neutral aspects of Planets identified.

There are also temporary relationships that occur as well. Typically, you can identify certain Houses as being friends and other Houses as being enemies on a temporary basis. These are the relationships that will vary greatly based upon an individual's specific birth chart and will have greater variance. When you want to look at temporary relationships, you will need to look at the placements of Planets in the following Houses:

Temporary friends: These are Planets in the second, third, fourth, tenth, eleventh, and twelfth Houses.

Temporary enemies: These are Planets in the fifth, sixth, seventh, eighth, or ninth Houses.

If you want to be able to identify the temporary relationships on a chart, you would look to see what the signs are normally, as well as the current temporary sign relationship. So, if you wanted to identify the relationship between the Sun and Moon, you would note that on a permanent level, the Sun and Moon are friends. However, based upon the placement of the House, this could change. If the Sun is in the fifth House, it may temporarily be an enemy.

When you are comparing the different Planets together, you will realize that you can have different combinations based upon how the permanent and temporary relationships combine. Consider these different conditions:

Permanent and temporary enemy: This is defined as a *great enemy*.

Permanent neutral and temporary enemy: This is defined as an *enemy*.

Permanent enemy and temporary friend: This is defined as *neutral*.

Permanent neutral and temporary friend: This is defined as a *friend*.

Permanent friend and temporary friend: This is defined as a *great friend*.

This helps you to identify the chart. If you find that your Sun is in a friend House, you will realize that it is currently a great friend, and as a result, you will realize that you've got a good chance at happiness. You will also be able to read these in other manners, which we will get to more when we discuss the different signs in Vedic astrology. There are all sorts of other factors that come into play here as well.

COMBUSTION OF PLANETS

Planets cannot get too close to the Sun, or they begin to get weak. When they are too close to the sun, their influence and power are typically weakened. When a Planet gets too close to the sun, it is said to combust. This is problematic, though you may want to consider that Venus and Mercury are always close to the Sun in the first place.

When Planets combust, they usually influence the Houses that they rule. For example, if Venus is combusted while ruling the seventh House, it may cause problems with the relationships that are had. Let's go over the idea of lording Houses and what happens when their Planets combust:

Combustion of First Lord: Weakened health

- **Combustion of Second Lord**: Weakened familial relationships

- **Combustion of Third Lord:** Struggles for younger siblings

- **Combustion of Fourth Lord:** Struggles for mother

- **Combustion of Fifth Lord:** Struggles with having children or with them

- **Combustion of Sixth Lord:** Troubles with subordinates and with the immune system or resistance to sickness

- **Combustion of Seventh Lord:** Problems in relationships or marriage

- **Combustion of Eighth Lord:** Problems with longevity

- **Combustion of Ninth Lord:** Problems with the father

- **Combustion of Tenth Lord:** Problems with authority figures

- **Combustion of Eleventh Lord:** Problems with older siblings

THE PLANETS (GRAHAS) | 73

- **Combustion of Twelfth Lord:** Problems with feeling loss or isolated

As you can see, Planets, which have combusted typically highly influence the connection and relationships that you have with those around you. Typically, Planets within an 8-degree radius of the Sun wind up combusting, and the closer that you get to the sun, the more likely that you are to see that your Planet has combusted and the more prominent the effects will become. Keep in mind that if the Sun combusts a Planet that is already malefic, the effects can become much worse as well.

RETROGRADE PLANETS

Finally, the last point to consider is what happens to Planets when they are in retrograde. You've probably heard this before, but you may not know what is meant. This occurs because all Planets move at a different speed relative to the Earth. Sometimes, Planets can appear to become stationary in their orbit, or even appear to backtrack in their orbit due to the distance and the speed at which the Earth and that Planet are both moving. When the Planet appears to be moving backward, it is referred to as the retrograde. The Sun and Moon never move in retrograde, but other Planets can.

When in retrograde, the effects of that Planet are pushed inward—they become internal, and while this can be disadvantageous in certain situations, it is also useful if you are trying to internalize your feelings as well. However, when you have several different Planets in retrograde, you may have negative thoughts during that period of time.

However, Mercury and Venus do not often find themselves impacted by retrograde. They can move toward the Sun toward combustion, or they can move away from the sun. Typically, effects are worse when they retrograde toward the Sun, and as a result, you can run into all sorts of other problems. In particular, it is unfavorable to have your Planet impacted by the retrograde while also under other negatives, such as combustion or being in a malefic House. The effects can compound onto each other and cause extra problems for you.

Typically, malefics when retrograding tend to cause extra problems. They limit you more or cause problems that you will have to overcome in some way. However, benefics falling into retrograde lose their usefulness or become unreliable, especially if they are also impacted by combustion.

Typically, Planets that are in retrograde in the birth chart are indicative of karmic influences and reveal much about the past life. Mercury, in particular, will show that you have been influenced in a past life, and as a result, you may find yourself struggling with speech.

When a Planet comes to be in retrograde on a birth chart, you will need to look closely at its temporary and permanent relationships. You will see that karma typically is able to work itself through the retrograde, and when you are dealing with retrograde Planets, you probably have a lot of unresolved karmic problems that you will need to deal with. Malefics and retrograde Planets reveal key information about what your karma looked like in the past so that you can then begin to deal with everything that went wrong.

If you need to interpret this, then, you can understand that people with many retrogrades typically have plenty of karma that they have to work through. They show signs of needing to learn lessons related to them, especially when in malefic Houses. However, your benefic Houses typically provide you with the tools that you will need to help you with those lessons.

CHAPTER 5:
THE ZODIACAL SIGNS

There are twelve astrological signs in Vedic astrology, just as you can see in Western astrology. These are the same signs, though they will have their own names. Each sign is roughly 30 degrees in the span. They begin with Aries and end with Pisces. As you read through this chapter, you will learn more about each of the Zodiacal signs so that you can better understand them and their lore. Typically, they are assigned by nature and have their own distinct characteristics and meanings.

The Zodiac is what most people think of when they are referring to in astrology. However, remember—we are looking at the position of the signs on the eastern horizon at the moment of your birth—this means that you are not going to have the same sign all day long or all month long, as you would in Western astrology.

Within this chapter, we are going to address several different aspects of the various signs. You will learn about what they mean, how they are interpreted, and how they can influence the individual as well. They are all quite different in nature, varying in their dualities, triplicities, and quadruplicities. By the end of this chapter, you will better understand this concept and be able to better direct your attention where it belongs. By learning to do this accordingly, you will realize that you can better control the way in which you interact with your own birth charts and readings.

76 | VEDIC ASTROLOGY

In the picture below, you will see the twelve Zodiac signs. In order from left to right, top to bottom, they are Aries, Taurus, Gemini, Cancer, Leo, Virgo, Libra, Scorpio, Sagittarius, Capricorn, Aquarius, and Pisces.

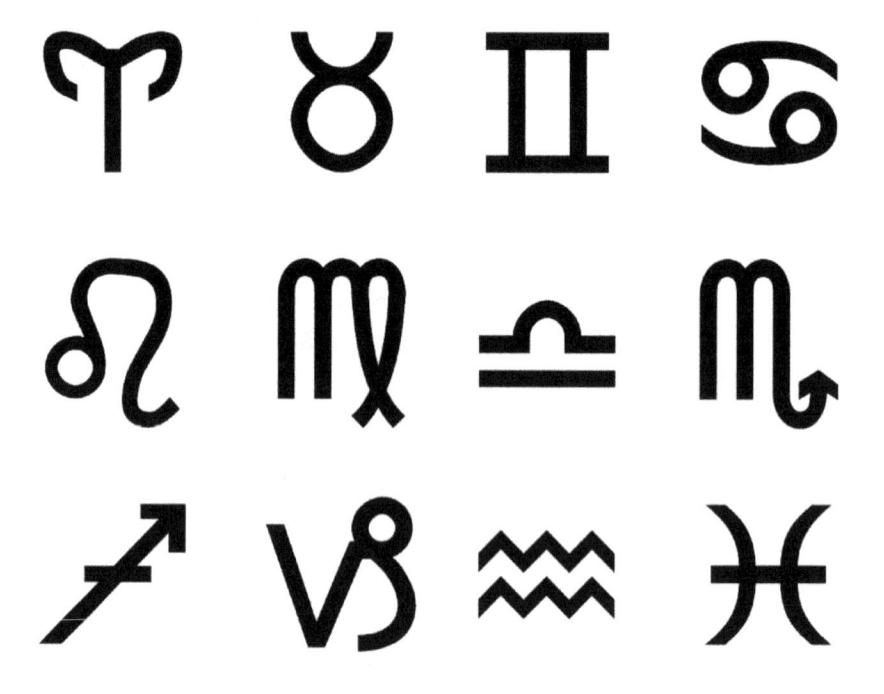

DUALITIES AND THE ZODIAC

The signs are divided up between two traits—they can be positive or negative. Positive signs are dubbed masculine, while the negative signs are feminine. The positive signs are day signs—they are representative of odd-numbered signs, as well as positive and air or fire. On the other hand, even signs are deemed negative and feminine, indicative of nighttime.

Effectively, all fire and air signs will be deemed positive, masculine, and relevant to the daytime. On the other hand, you can expect feminine, negative, and night signs to be all of the earth and water signs. Between the two, all positive signs are extroverted, while the negative tend to be introverted.

TRIPLICITIES AND THE ZODIAC

Perhaps one of the most important points of considerations for astrology is the type that it is. This is done by the element, which can then describe the temperament and personality of the sign as well. For predictive purposes, you can then begin to identify their signs and tendencies. Each element will have three signs that are put to it. The elements in Vedic astrology are Fire, Water, Earth, and Air. These are triplicities in the fact that they divide the elements into groups of three.

Fire signs

Fire signs are defined as being fiery in both mind and spirit. They are willing to burn with the activity and confidence that they imbue. The element of fire is recognized as being the defining of Aries, Leo, and Sagittarius. Additionally, it presides over the First, Fifth, and Ninth Houses. Those who are of the Fire element are seen as active and spirited. They are confident in their endeavors, recognizing that they have the power to take action and make real change. They are outgoing in their pursuits and are typically also quite comfortable in adventure, exhibiting plenty of enthusiasm and optimism.

On the other hand, however, they are notably impatient in their actions. They are willful and reactive as well—if they do not like something, they are much more likely to take action than anything else. They will react to conflict aggressively and are typically overly blunt and careless in their responses. When you have Planets or Houses with these signs, you will note that they will take on the fiery temperament of this element.

Water signs

Water is indicative of imagination and feelings. It embraces the signs of Cancer, Scorpio, and Pisces, and also the Fourth, Eighth, and Twelfth Houses. Those who fall in these Houses typically find themselves sensitive and kind. They are domestic in their endeavors and typically sympathize well. They are compassionate and benevolent, recognizing that they can also be artistic and intuitive as well. They are creative individuals that are willing to embrace this attitude to their fullest extent—they are willing to embody that creativity.

However, Water is also typically associated with moodiness and clinginess. The individuals can be quite secretive if they need to and find that they are typically broody. They may have their own unrealistic interpretations of the world around them, and they may run into problems with this.

Earth signs

The Earth signs are Aries, Leo, and Sagittarius, and the Houses represented are the Second, Sixth, and Tenth. These signs are typically noted as being responsible and steadfast. They are naturally reliable, organized, practical, ambitious, realistic, and hardworking in their endeavors. They are typically able to get through their work with an analytical note, and they are willing to do whatever it takes to succeed and complete their goals or responsibilities.

THE ZODIACAL SIGNS | 79

On the negative end of the spectrum, however, they tend to be quite stubborn. Typically, you can see them as lazy and critical as well—they will fuss and be quite pessimistic and elitist. They see the negative side of things regularly.

Air signs

Finally, let's consider the air signs. These are those of Gemini, Libra, and Aquarius. They are also the natural Third, Seventh, and Eleventh Houses. The signs are indicative of mental and social lives—they are those that are willing to communicate and are typically quick of wit. The air signs are just as flexible as the air itself and are able to adapt to just about any situation with their flexibility. They are usually quite focused on their relationships and are willing to do what they can to do make it work in them. They are typically quite tolerant of their existence and are willing to do what they can to make sure that they are able to stand for themselves.

However, they can also be nervous or even superficial. They can get caught up on the wrong detail and wind up, focusing far too much on it. Sometimes, they may get stuck trying to make a decision and not knowing what to do with it—they are stuck in trying to figure out how to get by. They may also be aloof and distant.

QUADRUPLICITIES AND THE ZODIAC

Additionally, each sign has a quadruplicity as well—these are the ways that they approach situations—they may be cardinal, fixed, or mutable. This determines what the individuals are likely to deal with things at the moment. These are signs that have been grouped into fours. They are used with the elemental Triplicities to better define each sign that exists. Now, let's take a look at the three quadruplicities.

Cardinal (movable) signs

Cardinal signs, Aries, Cancer, Libra, and Capricorn, are those that move. They are willing to change and grow as necessary—

they are enterprising, and those under this quadruplicity will have no qualms about setting up change. In fact, they will usually welcome and embrace change, even going so far as encouraging it if they need to. They enjoy being able to invoke change and create novelty in the world. Typically, these are people who dislike being stuck in a subservient role—they thrive best when they are able to take charge to create the changes that they want. However, on the other hand, they may become quite restless if they are stuck.

Fixed (static) signs

Fixed signs, Taurus, Leo, Scorpio, and Aquarius, are those that are focused on what they are doing at any point in time. They are patient, determined, and they have the stamina to continue toward their goals at all costs. They will be persistent toward those causes that they choose to push. When they finally get their mind on something, they fixate on it and will chase it down endlessly until they are able to get it. They are quite rigid in terms of their attitude and usually will not change their opinions. However, on the other hand, they can be resistant to being presented with change, and they may struggle with their decision making. Additionally, they may find that their stubbornness and tenacity, which can be highly beneficial in some contexts, is actually their worst enemy at times. Their unwillingness to budge or give in to other people can make them dangerous.

Mutable (common) signs

Finally, the mutable signs, Gemini, Virgo, Sagittarius, and Pisces, are those that are easily adaptable. They are willing to change as necessary and will flex and give if that is what the situation calls for. They are described as balanced between the signs that they are in. They will adapt as necessary to their current situation and change as desired. However, as good as it can be that they are flexible, that flexibility can also cost them dearly as well. They can be quite indecisive and even vacillating at times, and that can make them difficult to get along with.

ARIES: CARDINAL FIRE *(MESH)*

Most compatible: *Leo, Sagittarius*

Somewhat compatible: *Aries, Gemini, Libra, Aquarius*

Least compatible: *Taurus, Cancer, Virgo, Scorpio, Capricorn, Pisces*

Aries is the first of the Zodiacal signs. It is represented by the constellation of a ram, with the sign being represented by the horns of the ram. In the sky, it is from 0 degrees up to 29. The Sun is in Aries from April 14 to May 14 in Vedic astrology. It is ruled by Mars, making it responsible for the head and brain, and it is also the First House in the horoscope. Typically, it is related to high levels of vitality and strength, alongside courage and a strong will. This particular sign is recognized as being indicative of the beginning, but also impulse and initiation.

It is the point of beginning, and when your Sun is in Aries, you will see that you are capable of creating a new sense of self. Your energies during this time are focused on you and you alone. You will have to be careful to avoid pushing ahead unnecessarily. Typically, those ruled by Aries are willing to take authority whenever possible, and they will work hard to inspire those around them. They naturally want to be that person in their group, and with their unending energy and willing to risk things, they are quite good at it.

However, they may struggle with some negatives as well—some Arians find themselves too self-centered or focused inwardly, and as a result, it can be easy to forget what they are actually trying to do. They can be difficult in relationships or as employees because they want to lead.

TAURUS: FIXED EARTH *(RISHABH)*

This sign of the Zodiac is represented by the bull. Its sign is the bull's head and horns, and it is from 30 degrees to 59 degrees in the sky. It is typically defined as from May 15 to June 14 in Vedic astrology. This sign is ruled by Venus and is highly influenced as such. It is typically deemed to be earthly and feminine, and it is able to govern over the throat. This second House of the horoscope is known for its endurance. Additionally, it is recognized by the stability that it represents and the desire to stick to sensuality and tradition. Typically, you can use Taurus to represent a desire toward success, ambition, and fertility.

This sign represents production, as well as money. Typically, these people put plenty of emphasis on their personal items because they do not feel comfortable or secure if they do not have objects of their own to hold onto. This can be a major problem for them—they can get too drawn to needing physical possessions, but it can also drive them to be productive. These people usually are found working at slower paces, but they will do what they can to finish what they begin. This allows them the trustworthiness that Taurus is known for.

Typically, these people are not easy to anger, but when they are, they will stick to that anger for a long while afterward. They are talented in being able to give advice to others, giving them that sense of security.

GEMINI: MUTABLE AIR *(MITHUN)*

The third sign is Gemini. This sign is represented by twin children, and the symbol is two vertical and two horizontal lines so that it can create the look of duality. It is located between 60 degrees to 80 degrees, and the Sun is present in Gemini from June 15 to July 15, based upon Vedic astrology.

Ruled by Mercury, this sign is responsible for governing the lungs, the hands, and the third House. It is flexible and intellectual. In particular, it is well-known for analytical thinking as well as various interests of communication. It is also quite representative of the idea of dualities, with two twins. It is necessary for the analysis of goals, self-analysis, and value, alongside with the environment and traveling.

Gemini is a person who enjoys a variety. To them, variety is truly the spice of life, and they prefer to work in ways that will grant them the ability to travel or achieve that mental stimulation that they are looking for. This usually makes them jump from thing to thing without much consistency because they constantly want to find that next new opportunity that is better than the last. Typically, these people are more perceptive and intuitive, and they can pair that with rationality. This is essential for them, and it is one of their best benefits.

However, because they are so quick to pick up too many activities all at once, they can wind up late in finishing up their projects. They can also see both sides of a situation, which means that they can get stuck in their minds for too long. This is another problem that they can run into. Additionally, they tend to stick to the use of logic and reason over emotionality, which can also become a problem and make them seem even fickle at times. They struggle with concentration, but when they are able to harness their mind just right, they can become a master of many instead of a jack of all trades, but master of none.

CANCER: CARDINAL WATER (*KARKA*)

This sign is the fourth in the Zodiac, symbolized by a crab. In terms of the symbol that is written, it is the breasts. This particular sign starts at 90 degrees all the way to 119 degrees, and the Sun is within Cancer from July 16 to August 16. This particular sign is known as being related to being able to feel for support, as well as maintenance. It is responsible for traditionalism and the focus of the family. It is necessary for the understanding of introversion, but still being nurturing at the same time.

Cancers usually enjoy being able to connect to the sea or working to help support other people domestically. They are the happiest working through the world with their emotions, and they tend to be highly sensitive to the emotional world around them. They typically find that they support the people around them, but they also seek out sympathy for themselves as well without recognizing that they do.

For Cancers, they struggle to create purpose. Like emotions, their purposes can come and go, and they may make sudden decisions without rhyme or reason that could be discerned by someone, not in their heads. They love focusing on being at home, looking at their family life, and focusing upon it. However, they are also perfectly content traveling. Typically, they work hard and without expectation of thanks for their family. They value making sure that their family is safe at all costs.

However, Cancers tend to worry. They are typically likely to allow their worries to be kept to themselves, and for this problem, they can run into stress-related ailments such as ulcers. Typically, they keep their emotions inward—they don't see the purpose in showing emotion outwardly, but they do have a tendency to project without realizing it.

LEO: FIXED FIRE (*SIMHA*)

This sign is most notable in the stars as a head of the lion, and the symbol is drawn by the mane of the lion. It is from 120 degrees to 149 degrees, and the Sun is in Leo from August 17 to September 16, based on Vedic astrology. In particular, this sign is defined closely by self-consciousness, dominance, focusing on realizing one's true self, and courage. Additionally, it can be linked to lively vitality, creativity, and even egocentrism if allowed to go too far. Typically, it focuses upon the building of one's personality and goals, along with finally achieving one's own self-realization.

Typically, Leos at work find that they are highly creative. They work in ways that will tap into their ability to be creative and capable of being able to exploit their own strengths. Typically, they are highly cheerful and even optimistic, and they will typically bring brightness to those around them. They are usually generous, and may even find that they have a penchant for dramatics and storytelling. They love to be the center of attention and enjoy themselves. Typically, they will focus on athletics and theater, and they tend to look toward the bigger picture and how they can get what they want, even if it is not necessarily affordable or realistic. Despite this, they are typically seen as lively and in good health, and they typically recover easily without much of a problem when they are ill.

Unfortunately, Leos make for poor leaders. They may be courageous and willing to be in the center of everything, but the problem is that they typically do not want to go through the paperwork or other boring duties that would go into it. Though not really susceptible to depression, when it gets bad enough, their depression can be completely debilitating, but thankfully, they can usually recover again relatively quickly. Another negative trait common to Leo is that end to cling to opinions; they are very closed-minded and refuse both emotional and rational attempts to change their thought processes.

VIRGO: MUTABLE EARTH (*KANYA*)

Virgo is the sixth sign and is represented by a virgin. The symbol is that of the maiden, and t is recognized from 150 degrees to 179. The Sun is in Virgo from September 17 to October 16. It is recognized as being able to secure over perfection, criticality, and more. Those ruled by Virgo tend to be detail-oriented, focusing on how they are able to interpret them. They are oftentimes practical and able to work toward their goals well. The sign of Virgo represents being able to understand and achieve goals, as well as the instinct for self-criticism.

Those ruled by Virgo are highly inquisitive and tend to have sharp memories and analytical skills. They typically enjoy spending time analyzing their issues in life, and they are driven by being able to recognize the where, when, how, and why. They are eager to work hard and ensure that they are able to be practical while also detail-oriented. They can make the most of their nervous energy, and they tend to get themselves involved in all sorts of activities. They are quick to be driven to nervousness, and their struggle to relax can cause them some struggles. However, they are able to be dependable with their own organization and scheduling. They will attempt to create perfection as much as possible, and they may become critical in an attempt to fix the problem.

Typically, Virgos are kind and dislike struggling and argument. They would rather be quiet and gentle than attempt to do anything else. Typically, you will find that they are quite likely to show signs of worry, and that can translate to almost becoming a hypochondriac. However, they are also quite healthy, so this is not usually a concern.

LIBRA: CARDINAL AIR (*TULA*)

This sign is the seventh in the Zodiac and is identified by the pairs of scales. The symbol for Libra is the Sun as it sets halfway beyond the horizon. It is from 180 degrees to 209 degrees, and the Sun is in Libra from October 17 to November 15 in Vedic astrology. This sign is all about harmony and balance. It is about finding that line between pleasure and working together, as well as symbolizing the relationships with other people and the goals that you have with regard to others.

Those who are Libras find themselves often deemed to be thoughtful, and their penchant for balance becomes obvious in their need to be excellent hosts to their guests. Typically, just being in their home reveals that they care deeply for a need for harmony as they work—it shows that they are able to balance things out. Libras struggle on their own—they need someone that they can share their life with, and because of that, they may rush to fall in love because they love the idea of being in love. Their need for romance and sentiment can have them rushing right into a relationship without meaning to, and that can be a huge problem for them.

Unfortunately, they often find that it is impossible to be emotionally stable if the world around them is currently rocking, and they will not stop at anything if it means that they can achieve that peace that they were looking for. The Libras of the world desire peace at all costs, and if they find that there is emotional turmoil around them, they will struggle to find their own emotional stability. For them, they will find that they get stuck in indecisiveness that they will need to be mindful of—it is one of their greatest hurdles. Additionally, they must be mindful to avoid falling trap to other people changing their opinions. While they may be creative, they are also very cerebral—they can live in their minds, and though this is not always seen, they prefer to take charge, albeit with caution. They work toward their goals, and when they want something done, they can make it happen.

SCORPIO: FIXED WATER (*VRISCHIKA*)

The eighth sign of the Zodiac is Scorpio. It is represented by the scorpion, and its symbol is that of male fertility. It is from 210 degrees to 239 degrees in the sky, and the Sun is within Scorpio from November 16 to December 15, based on Vedic astrology. This Planet is mystical in personality and is known for having strong, passionate emotions. Scorpios are known for their transcendental drive and their passion and depth. The personality that they represent is recognized as being self-destructive and transcends the limitations of any sort of physical existence. Scorpios strive to achieve an existence that is able to transcend their physical sieves—they want to be more than their self-consciousness.

This is one of the most powerful of the signs thanks to their strength of emotion and their hardheaded goal to constantly strive to succeed at all costs. They are highly influenced by their mind, which is analytical in nature, and yet they also possess a powerful sense of intuition that they are able to rely upon. They are skilled at not only reasoning with those around them, but also with being able to perceive the world around them. They are able to come up with their own opinions because of this, and it is usually incredibly difficult to get them to change their minds. They will lose all sense of judgment if they find themselves criticisms, and they will become unwilling to admit that they may be wrong. They will do whatever it takes to protect that sense of what they've decided upon. Additionally, anything that they do must be important—they are born by the idea of trivialities, and they will not do anything that they think is not important enough.

Scorpios are quite stubborn, and when faced with attack or threat, they may find themselves feeling drawn to reacting with aggression, choosing both silence and sarcasm as weapons that they can use against other people. Their need for protecting their own beliefs can be difficult, and they will sit in their desire for vindication for a long period of time.

It is nearly impossible to deceive these people—their intuition will usually key them into the idea that someone has attempted to deceive them. As soon as they are aware of this, they are willing to do whatever it takes to overcome it.

SAGITTARIUS: MUTABLE FIRE (*DHANUS*)

This sign is noted by the symbol of a figure of a centaur—someone that is half horse and half man, typically with a bow and arrow. As such, he is typically represented with the symbol of an arrow. Sagitarrius is in the sky from 240 degrees to 269 degrees, and the Sun is in it from December 16 to January 13 in Vedic astrology. This particular sign is recognized by its love for philosophy and development of the mind. Additionally, it is closely aligned with optimism, a sense of worship for religion, and mysticism. Typically, it can be seen as indicative of intelligence and learning.

Those ruled by Sagittarius are typically outspoken, and even blunt at times. Their desire for the truth typically makes them speak before thinking—they will blurt out what they think. Of course, that bluntness can get them into trouble sometimes, but usually, thanks to the type of person that Sagittarians are, they can usually get away with it without much of a problem. People tend to be attracted to Sagittarius, and that attraction allows for them to be well-received, even though their comments at times can be harsh.

Typically, Sagittarians are quite interested in athletics, and they may find themselves watching and optimistically cheering for their teams of choice. They typically find that they are constantly looking for something to add more depth to their lives. They are willing to find those sources of happiness, but they can also find themselves quickly overextended and with too much to do. This can lead to them feeling overextended in many senses, and they can also find that they are quickly exhausted. Additionally, they may find that they give in to consuming too much food or drink as a result of their desire for enjoyment.

These people do not feel comfortable sitting down for long—they grow quite restless if left to their own devices, and that drive to do something can push them immensely. They may find that they are quite independent and find that they would do just about anything to avoid relationships. They dislike the idea of marriage—it can feel suffocating, and they can find themselves feeling restless in a relationship.

CAPRICORN: CARDINAL EARTH (*MAKARA*)

Capricorn is the tenth of the Zodiac signs and is depicted as a sea-goat. Typically, the symbol that is drawn shows a goat with a horn that has been twisted about. It can be found from 270 degrees up to about 299 degrees. The Sun is within Capricorn from January 14 to February 12 in Vedic astrology.

Typically this sign is recognized for the yearning for the top. Those who are Capricorns are constantly working on getting to the top, to realize their truest sense. They are typically able to show themselves, with ambition, who they are, and work to achieve something. It represents the ability to combine that sense of personal and absolute while letting go of the personal world and materialism. It is the utmost sense of pragmatism and a drive to make progress toward it.

The Capricorns in the world are constantly looking to see as much as possible before passing judgment. They like to be as rational as possible—they are constantly looking for the right decision based upon this sort of decision making. They will do whatever they can and are typically dependable, especially when they are needed the most. They are not typically aggressive, though they may be more aggressive in defensive behaviors if necessary. They are quick to recognize that they need people, but they are also afraid of being hurt in the process, meaning that they have a tendency to pull away and isolate themselves out of that fear. They are selective in who they want to be their friends, and they are usually quite conservative in how they think and with what they value. They believe that law and order matter, and they are highly respectful of tradition. It is something that they find to be unusual when it comes to adopting their own ideas. They are typically organized by nature, and they will possess the potential to be great in leadership, especially when they are able to maintain their self-discipline. They are willing to push toward success that they need, and they will give up things in order to achieve their goals, but they run the risk of exhausting themselves as well. However, they are more than willing to endure the hardships if they think that it will give them their goals.

AQUARIUS: FIXED AIR (*KUMBHA*)

Aquarius is the eleventh of the signs in the Zodiac. Represented by the Water-bearer, this sign is symbolized with the saves of water. It is from 300 degrees up to 329 degrees in the sky, and the Sun is in Aquarius from February 13 to March 14 in Vedic astrology. It is recognized for its attitude toward agreeability, originality, and being progressive. Aquarius is a freedom-loving member of the Zodiac and is recognized for the intellectual and spiritual values. It is something that is able to represent the next step toward transcending personal boundaries to create a universal or communal self and community.

These people are able to attract others despite their enigmatic personality types. They are strange due to the fact that they do not quite follow any of the known patterns, but they are also usually described as friendly and able to detach from those around them. They are warm but distant at the same time. Typically, they are focused more on the communal group than individual people. They are driven by their desire for novelty and achieving the success and comfort that they believe is needed in the world. They are driven to learn about art, science, literature, and even politics, in hopes of generating positive benefits, and they are typically highly powerful when it comes to being able to do so. They are great when it comes to concentrating, and they are likely able to assimilate the information that they learn. However, at the same time, they are able to have an almost absentminded attitude—they are stubborn but also willing to contrarily rebel just for fun. They are not willing to be intimidated or frightened, but at the same time, they will not allow themselves to be taken advantage of. They will intentionally shock people if they feel the need to, and they are willing to flip structures on their heads if they need to. They are willing to deliberately shock others, and typically, they reject the notion of schedules or rules. They are not willing to be found and controlled by rules, and though they may have many acquaintances, only a few are referred to as good friends. They typically do not concern themselves with what other people think, and as such, they tend to avoid forming opinions on what other people do.

PISCES: MUTABLE WATER (*MEENA*)

Finally, the last Zodiac sign is that of Pisces—the twelfth of the signs. It is represented by fish that are actively swimming apart from each other in two directions, and their sign is indicative of this, showing two fish with a line connecting the two together. In the sky, it is from 330 degrees and up to 359 degrees. The Sun is in Pisces from March 15 to April 13, according to the sidereal Zodiac in Vedic astrology. It is represented by complete transcendence from the material world, along with being ruled by one's own unwavering values. It is shown to be linked to impracticality along with spirituality all in one, along with the idea of self-sacrifice and empathy. It is designed to symbolize the ending of being confined in the world, recognizing that you can become one with the absolute, binding to the ocean, the sea, and the subconscious.

Those aligned with Pisces are self-sufficient and creative. They are willing to do what it takes to recognize that they are complex, and they are able to absorb knowledge about the world rather than being driven to learn it. They are highly active mentally and always willing to do what they can to self-sacrifice. They will empathize well with other people, and they are able to break free of the material to merge with the universe. They are naturally complex, friendly, adaptable, and versatile, but that comes with the caveat that they are also able to be influenced. They know when they are being deceived, but they also are not very strong when it comes to being steadfast in their choices. Their adaptability can lead to insecurity when they start to look for reassurance externally from other people instead of counting on themselves to be internally motivated. They are sensitive, gentle, and usually driven by their reluctance to get into confrontations. They can get dragged into situations that are emotional and find that they can't get out—they know what is happening but find that they are stuck.

Effectively, their biggest strength, that sacrificing and adaptable nature, becomes their weakness when they find that they can't get their way out of trouble; they find that they are stuck feeling emotionally driven and relating to other people. They can be great and live in peace, but it requires them to become willing to be steadfast.

CHAPTER 6:
THE HOUSES (*BHAVAS*)

Every person's birth chart can be broken down into twelve Houses. Within those Houses, different Planets can be placed, as you saw when we looked at birth charts. We spent a bit of time looking at them in earlier chapters, but have not yet sat down to really go over the true significance of the Houses and why they matter so much. Remember, the Houses judge everything. All matters in your life will be controlled and influenced by the Houses and what may or may not be within them. You will want to look to your Houses to better understand what is going on and how to begin planning your life. However, these Houses also do not exist within a vacuum either—they influence each other, as we will address within this chapter.

The horoscope is nothing more than a diagram built to show the world as seen from Earth. It is a chart that divides up the sky into twelve equal parts. These are the Houses in Vedic astrology. There are 12, and this is one of the three essential tools if you want to be able to identify a horoscope. To begin, you must recognize that there are always going to be six Houses above the horizon and six below. At the point of birth, you will see that House 1 begins on the easternmost point, just beneath the horizon. This is known as the ascendant. The point directly overhead is the divide between the ninth and tenth Houses. The point on the western horizon divides the sixth and seventh Houses.

This means, of course, that you can only ever see the seventh through twelfth Houses at any point in time. Thanks to the rotation of the Earth, you will notice that the Planets appear to rise in the east and set in the west. As you will see in the chart below, the horizon line is drawn in a thick black line across the chart, reflecting exactly that. The Sun will always rise from the east and set in the west as well.

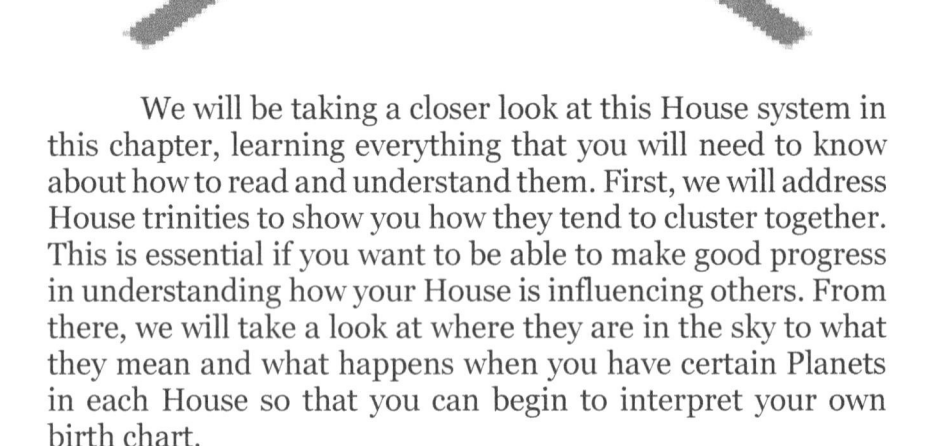

We will be taking a closer look at this House system in this chapter, learning everything that you will need to know about how to read and understand them. First, we will address House trinities to show you how they tend to cluster together. This is essential if you want to be able to make good progress in understanding how your House is influencing others. From there, we will take a look at where they are in the sky to what they mean and what happens when you have certain Planets in each House so that you can begin to interpret your own birth chart.

By the time that you are done reading through this chapter, you should have a good idea of the Houses and how significant they are. You should also be able to understand more or less how to expect certain readings to pan out for individuals, as well as get more information that you will need to read charts for both yourself and for others.

TRINITIES OF THE HOUSES

Before we begin to get into the details about the Houses themselves, let's take a look at the four trinities that exist within them. These are trios of Houses that are all related—they all influence each other closely and will create impacts upon each other. They are also related to the Triplicities that we looked at in Chapter 5. You will see that each trinity refers to one of the elements of the Zodiac as well.

Trinity of Dharma (1, 5, 9)

Your first, fifth, and ninth Houses all relate to the Fire signs. Aries is the first, Leo is the fifth, and Sagittarius is the ninth, and all three of these fire signs are related to very important parts of your body. Aries is related to the body, while Leo is related to the heart, and Sagittarius is related to the higher mind. These three work together to influence each other and are related to spiritual action.

Trinity of Artha

Next, the second, sixth, and tenth Houses all relate to each other as well. These are each related to the Earth signs—Taurus, Virgo, and Capricorn, respectively. These three signs are related to possessions, comforts, and honor. Together, they represent wealth overall, physically, and emotionally.

Trinity of Kama

The third trinity involves the third, seventh, and eleventh Houses. These three are represented by Air and involve Gemini, Libra, and Aquarius, respectively. They are related to the relationships that you have. Gemini relates to siblings, Libra relates to marriage, and Aquarius is related to friends and associates. When you look at the trinity of Kama, you learn all about the relationships that you will lead and how they will relate to each other.

Trinity of Moksha

Finally, let's consider the trinity of Moksha—this is the trinity of final liberation for the soul. These are the water signs, representing Cancer, Scorpio, and Pisces, which represent your environment, regeneration, and death, and suffering, respectively. Each of these will influence your path in life, relating closely to your karma.

CARDINAL, FIXED, AND MUTABLE HOUSES

Your Houses can be divided one more time into Cardinal, Fixed, and Mutable Houses. These have their own relationships and meanings that are essential to understand.

Cardinal Houses

Your Cardinal Houses are the pillars of any horoscope—they are the most important ones that will give you the main reading for the individual. You know this by looking at the First, Fourth, Seventh, and Tenth Houses.

Fixed Houses

The Fixed Houses include the Second, Fifth, Eighth, and Eleventh. They are related to money and material goods when you are trying to understand your reading. They are important for their own reasons.

Mutable Houses

Finally, the last four are your Mutable Houses. These are the Houses of decline. They include Third, Sixth, Ninth, and Twelfth.

FIRST HOUSE: ASCENDANT (*LAGNA OR TANU BHAVA*)

Significator: Sun

Zodiac: Aries

Body parts: Head, face, sensory organs

The First House is the most important one that you will read. It is referred to as "Tanu Bhava" in Vedic astrology, translating to "the House of the body." It is the birth point, recognizing the beginning of your very life. It is at that point that everything is created, and as such, this House is responsible for creating your looks, your body, your personality, and your general constitution. Remember, the Ascendant will always influence health, vitality, and disposition. It will also be important when determining how your life will generally go, looking at failures and successes, your fortune, and more. You will always start your reading here.

Sun in First House

When you have the Sun in this House, it is typically helpful, intensifying its vitality and working with its own attributes. It is going to bring happiness to the individual, and they will have a personality that is radiant like the sun. Typically, this is indicative of good health, a healthy constitution, and happiness as a child. The Sun will accentuate the positive aspects of the sign on the cusp of the ascendant. Typically, you will see that life will be successful in spirit and material. Typically, this individual will be prestigious and well-respected by their peers. They are likely to resist even the worst of circumstances or individuals that try to lead them astray.

Moon in First House

This implies that the emotional side of one's nature will be amplified. Typically, the individual will be timid and sensitive, but still ready to embrace change. Timidity will be their hurdle that must be overcome. The dualistic side of the individual is likely to be more pronounced, and personality is emphasized. This individual is more likely to travel and have a life seeking to be recognized and accepted by others.

Mercury in First House

This is highly related to the ability to express thoughts and ideas with ease. It is highly favorable and bodes well for the individual's intellect. They may travel often, and they prefer to communicate about travel. They may be restless, and that restlessness can hold them back at times. However, this is a good position for communication and expression. In retrograde, however, there may be problems with impatience, which will directly hold the individual back.

Venus in First House

Venus, as the Ascendant, shows that one is going to be a good companion. They will find that friendships and associations come easily. Typically, they will be happy, which aids them in overcoming negativity. You can usually expect these people to be artistic, hoping to find harmony and beauty in everything. They are typically blessed in beauty, charming, and naturally seductive, and are likely to seek jobs related to being satisfying aesthetically. In retrograde, however, they are likely to require attention and may even err on the side of egocentricity. They must make sure that they have that realistic attitude about themselves to keep them grounded.

Mars in first House

When Mars is Ascendant, typically, they will be strong and courageous. However, that can also exist alongside impulsiveness and anger. This will have to be overcome. Naturally assertive, these people may come across as almost boisterous and proud, dripping with enthusiasm. They are highly competitive. However, in retrograde, this can lead to problems with overconfidence and aggression. The individual's self-identity must be identified and balanced out.

Jupiter in First House

Jupiter in the First House is fortunate—it is the Planet of luck, and with this as your Ascendant, you will find that you are in a position of receiving those benefits. Even when things are problematic, you will realize that your main interests will be protected. Your optimism will be beneficial to you and help you to succeed. These people are likely to succeed, but when Jupiter is in retrograde, you may find that you rush forward without setting up your foundation first. You will find that you are highly independent, but also need to find truth in reality that you live.

Saturn in First House

With Saturn in the Ascendant, the individual is likely to be depressed or suffer from their health. However, they are also cautious and make it a point to think over their actions before moving forward. This is good, but can also be restrictive at time. This individual may suffer from procrastination just due to their own fear over moving forward. They will need to overcome this problem to succeed. They are likely to be diligent and serious. In retrograde, the individual will feel that there is a barrier blocking their connection to those around them. The individual will be sensitive and struggle to connect well.

Rahu in First House

In the first House, Rahu signs that the individual will value personal values more than the general public. They are reliant on only themselves and their own intuition. However, this can lead to problems as well. They may find that they struggle to connect well and that they will need to learn to make connections and work together. They must learn to work as part of a team.

Ketu in First House

With Ketu in the Ascendant, you will find that the individual feels a need to be with other people. Though independent by nature, it is essential for these people to find fulfillment in working to connect and cooperate with other people.

SECOND HOUSE (*DHANA BHAVA*)

Significator: *Venus and Jupiter*

Zodiac: *Taurus*

Body parts: *The right eye, teeth, tongue, nose, cheeks, neck and throat, chin*

The Second House is responsible for one's finances. In particular, it takes a look at how someone approaches money, earning it, and how it is used. If you look at the second House, you are considering how likely someone is to succeed financially or monetarily. It is imperative for making sure that the individual understands how to approach their wealth. It is not indicative of career, however—solely belongings, both physical and emotional. It will also influence one's inner self and family, as well. Immediate family is influenced by this House, and it will also influence how they tend to express themselves.

Sun in Second House

This individual is likely to be relatively successful, generous in nature, and probably happy enough. They are probably going to be recognized for the effort that they put out and will be beneficial. Money is gained through asserting oneself and being able to achieve an influential position. They are likely to gain respect from other people.

Moon in Second House

The Moon shows that there will be flexibility in one's income and expenditures. Typically, these people must be careful with the management of their money to make sure that they are relatively stable with their finances. If the Moon has a good aspect, they will likely see plenty of gains, but a negative aspect can cause problems, especially with extravagance and stability. Emotional stability must be learned to protect the individual's financial state.

Mercury in Second House

Mercury, in the second House, shows that financial interests will be directly related to intellect in some way, such as through literary pursuits or mental exercises. Money may naturally be made in those ways, and they may also show that they are generally successful with their financial affairs. This position will show an increase in concentration and memory, though in retrograde, this individual can become too defensive and even get stuck in a materialistic worldview.

Venus in Second House

When Venus is placed within the second House, you can expect a few different scenarios. If well aspected, the individual is likely to find that their influence that they have is highly beneficial, though, with a poor aspect, there is a good chance that there will be a detriment. Typically, earning will happen through fashion or beauty. In retrograde, however, the individual may find that they are materialistic and potentially even stingy.

Mars in Second House

When Mars is in this House, you may find that the individual is able to earn money through hard work. This individual is likely to take risks, and they make money as a result. They also, however, spend readily and heavily, and this can make saving difficult. In retrograde, however, there are strong desires that hold the individual back. They will give in recklessly to their wants, and as a direct result, they can end up unhappy with what they have.

Jupiter in Second House

In the second House, you will see Jupiter create good luck and fortune. This is highly beneficial to the individual. However, with a bad aspect, it could feature loss heavily. The individual is likely to be sympathetic and benevolent, and though he or she may have a great judgment with money, a bad aspect can ruin this. In retrograde, there is a focus on hedonism and materialism that can be difficult to overcome.

Saturn in Second House

Saturn positioned here will show that the individual is likely to experience plenty of financial anxiety. They may struggle with making financial plans, and as a result, the individual must take the time to get to know how to relax. Patience must be cultivated, and the individual must learn to persevere through hardships financially. The individual may find that they struggle with finances and find that they are underpaid for all of their efforts. In retrograde, the individual is often stuck to old values and will not make changes that are necessary.

Rahu in Second House

Rahu, in the second House, usually signifies that there are strange financial abilities. The individual must become capable of standing on their own feet and working with their own resources. They may find that they instinctively lean on other people for help, but they must learn to fulfill themselves. Avoid credit as much as possible.

Ketu in Second House

With Ketu in the Second House, you will find that finances must change somehow. Instead of focusing on the material, the individual will discover that there is more to life and the world than just having possessions. They can be enhancers in life, but they should not be the sole purpose. These individuals have a tendency to get tuck on personal resources and fail to develop accordingly.

THIRD HOUSE (BUDDHI BHAVA)

Significator: Mercury

Zodiac: Gemini

Body parts: Right ear, hands, arms, shoulder blade, collar bone, respiratory system, nervous system

This House is indicative of one's ability to communicate with others. Additionally, it relates to the individual's journeys in life, as well as their younger siblings, along with their neighbors. It is also highly related to one's inner strength and thoughts that they have, whether they are courageous or able. This also links to memory and power and property of the mind.

Sun in Third House

This positioning of the Sun shows a desire to be communicative and to travel. The travel is meant to find influential people. Individuals with the Sun in Third tend to show that they are interested in intellect and studies. They are more likely to pursue something because of interest than for advancement. The Sun can create a magnanimous mind that is prideful and ambitious, firm, and independent, all at the same time. These people reach for success wherever they can get it.

Moon in Third House

The Moon, when positioned here, shows that the individual will travel often. They will likely find that they travel for personal endeavors, as well as for occupation. They will be imaginative and seek to gain and utilize knowledge in life. This individual is likely to travel regularly, struggle with education early on, but have a great attachment to siblings. They will tend to learn from absorbing information around them and are highly receptive to their surroundings.

Mercury in Third House

Mercury, in this position, is typically related to a strong desire to travel and seek variety. This individual will likely attempt to gain knowledge in as many ways as possible, though they can sometimes choose not to delve very deeply into it. As a result, they learn a superficial amount of knowledge without really understanding what they are looking at. This is Mercury's best position, and you will find that there is plenty of success. In retrograde, however, this individual is likely to find that they invest too much in attempting to be understood.

Venus in Third House

Venus, when in the Third House, is a great position for any relations to your neighbors or family members. There will be good, strong relationships built upon harmony here. They typically show that they have a high capacity for studying and art in general. They may also find that they are skilled in writing or lecturing. They find that they want to travel regularly. In retrograde, however, the individual is likely to require an analysis of one's love life to ensure that they are having meaningful contact with others.

Mars in Third House

Mars in this House can create a higher drive to travel, but also can lend itself to more accidents during this travel due to being put into dangerous situations during attempts to take risks. This individual is more likely to care about mechanics and is attracted to buildings or explosives. There is a desire for speed, strong relationships with close relatives, and high levels of influence available here. However, they may be aggressive as well. In retrograde, this individual becomes too direct and forceful and must be mindful of his surroundings while also not taking things too seriously.

Jupiter in Third House

Jupiter in the third House creates a strong desire for long-distance travel. The individual will gravitate toward exploration and adventure. They will find cheerfulness and optimism in their mindset as well. They will likely have good relationships with their family while also being lucky on journeys. In retrograde, they may find that they want to travel constantly without setting down roots. They should be able to communicate plenty without many words.

Saturn in Third House

This placement leads to forethought and concentration being tantamount. However, with the wrong aspects, the individual can suffer from depression. Their relationships may be wrought with anxiety and worry. These people tend to avoid traveling and withdraw. They are cautious in their lives. In retrograde, they can get stuck in seeing the world in black and white without seeing much in-between.

Rahu in Third House

This placement is linked to awareness in life and in a social setting. These individuals are typically aware of how they impact those around them. They will have great relationships with their siblings, and they will travel often. They may find that they are extreme in their beliefs sometimes.

Ketu in Third House

This individual often finds that they have a need to understand the world around them to be happy, and they pursue not only science but also philosophy and religion in hopes of broadening their horizons. They feel obligated to those around them, and though they may find that there are problems with relatives, they are willing to remain dutiful to them. They may find that they get so caught up in their religion that they can't listen to others.

FOURTH HOUSE (*BANDHU BHAVA*)

Significator: Moon

Zodiac: Cancer

Body parts: Chest, breasts, and the lungs

The Fourth House is essential to deciphering someone else's House and home, along with their mother, their domestics, and how likely that they are to acquire any tangible assets in their lives This could include land and buildings, or cars or even intangible happiness and knowledge. This House is called the womb often because of the fact that it is related to the mother and hidden secrets.

Sun in Fourth House

This particular position shows that all matters in domestics are intensified, whether good or bad. Usually, the individual is deeply involved when it comes to matters involving his or her family. The Sun will assist in ensuring that property is cared for and shows that earlier efforts will pay off in the future. This individual must focus on maintaining vitality and health in later years.

Moon in Fourth House

This is typically related to being bonded closely to one's mother. Usually, the individual will think of their mother in high regard, and they will strongly value their home ties. They tend to have an intense desire to find comfort in their home life, and they work to live peacefully. When that is not the case, they tend to fall into depression or anxiety as a direct result. This position indicates that the individual is more likely to focus on the latter part of their life.

Mercury in Fourth House

When Mercury gets this position, typically, it intensifies the individual's imagination and mind. The individual will seek out harmonious domestic life and will make great progress in both private and business endeavors. However, when there are problems on the home front, they may find that they are troubled greatly in all aspects. In retrograde, this individual finds that family is the most important circle, and they tend to be highly influenced by childhood.

Venus in Fourth House

This is a good spot to have Venus, and it is related to peace in family life. This is important in all aspects of life, gaining monetarily and socially when the family affairs are in order. Typically, this individual will make home life highly important. They usually have plenty of opportunities to have a secure marriage and home life. In retrograde, love will almost always take on a parental form.

Mars in Fourth House

Mars does not do well in this position, and the individual is likely to suffer domestically as a result. Typically, this can happen with the parents who may be high-strung. Home will not quite fit the picture that this individual wants, and as a result, they may find that they are happier leaving their birthplace entirely. In retrograde, this individual feels a need to be dominant over family, and they will need to be able to overcome this desire.

Jupiter in Fourth House

Jupiter in the Fourth House is usually good—it will bring happy family settings. Usually, the individual will find that they are able to benefit from their family members as well. So long as there is no bad aspect causing problems, the individual should see that the ending half of life should be pleasant emotionally and materially. In retrograde, there may be strong levels of emotion that can make it difficult to think clearly, and dwelling on these problems can become a concern.

Saturn in Fourth House

Saturn in the Fourth House is almost always bad. It leads to struggles in family life and can even cause problems with marriage if it happens. Usually, the individual will be caught up with their parents, leading to a lack of time for a relationship. Both the beginning and end of life will not be pleasant, and there will likely be struggles with relationships. In retrograde, the individual will be focused inwardly, and they must be able to learn to live in the present to manage their problems.

Rahu in Fourth House

When Rahu is in the Fourth House, there are usually benefits noted from parents, typically from the mother's side. Typically this comes through the real estate of some sort. Homelife will usually be significant. They may find that there are issues with early connections or feeling unloved early on. Career is not as important to these people as their home life, though they have an ego. They may not ever actually be prominent in their field, despite wanting to be.

Ketu in Fourth House

When Ketu is in the Fourth House, there is a deep need to find recognition through professional or personal achievements. Additionally, the individual will feel an innate drive to retreat away from society at large in an attempt to remain in their safety at home. They tend to be driven to share their talent outward and publically, and if they try to live their lives entirely at home, they tend to struggle and fail. They are able to uplift others through their inspiration, and they feel a need to do so.

FIFTH HOUSE (*PUTRA BHAVA*)

Significator: *Jupiter*

Zodiac: *Leo*

Body parts: *Heart, upper and middle spine*

This House is significant in showing someone's creativity levels. Additionally, it can be related to children as well as the virtue of a past life. It also relates back to romance and love, along with hobbies and sports as well. This House is recognized as determining if someone is able to have children while recognizing the conception of pregnancy. Additionally, it will show artistic tastes as well as pleasures.

Sun in Fifth House

The Sun in this House is favorable and will lead to forming good attachments to others. It also shows that you are likely to have male children. It is perfect if you are interested in pursuing acting or artistic ventures, and in early life, the individual will likely desire children. As one ages, they will become more interested in the next generation. He or she may end up helping younger individuals in life somehow.

Moon in Fifth House

Generally, this is associated with intense emotions and good love affairs or flirtation. Additionally, it is associated with female children primarily and shows creative potential, good judgment, and enterprising nature. Be cautious in a love affair. It tends to imply plenty of fertility and children.

Mercury in Fifth House

This is associated with optimistic outlooks mentally and the capacity for being able to combine intellect and art together. Knowledge is assimilated easily and passed on to others as well through teaching and instruction. It may show love affairs regularly, as well as any attachments. In retrograde, it may imply a need to sit down and think.

Venus in Fifth House

Venus in Fifth is a great position leading to strength and vitality within one's love life. There is a strong desire for love and companionship. Typically it shows favor toward female children and art. In retrograde, it can show creativity, sexuality, or having children as self-confirmation.

Mars in Fifth House

Mars in Fifth tends to show intense desire toward the opposite sex and passion that is difficult to control. It can sometimes be linked to troubles with attachments and breakups or having children out of wedlock. Typically, it favors problematic male children. In retrograde, there are typically struggles with communicating about sexuality and expression.

Jupiter in Fifth House

Jupiter in the Fifth House will show great benefits to the individual. It shows signs of good love attachments and benefits from those relationships. It typically shows that there will be love found through shared interests, a good influence over children, and mainly male offspring. In retrograde, the individual will have a dominating nature while also chasing after goals. However, they may also get too confident and overestimate themselves.

Saturn in Fifth House

This is associated with struggles in love and friendships. Typically this is due to a struggle with self-expression. This causes problems with family as well, and there are often struggles with raising children. These people tend to have problems reproducing or may not want to have children at all. In retrograde, this individual has obstacles that they want to overcome but may struggle to do so.

Rahu in Fifth House

This is typically associated with good relationships with children. Typically, this individual finds that love and affection work well. However, there may be some disappointing friendships along the way.

Ketu in Fifth House

When Ketu is in the Fifth House, you can find that there is a need to elevate goals to new levels that would be good for the entire group. This is essential to finding ways to succeed. They have great creative potential and need to learn to use them for the betterment of other people.

SIXTH HOUSE (*ARI BHAVA*)

Significator: Mercury

Zodiac: Virgo

Body parts: Pancreas, stomach, Intestinal tract, duodenum, digestive tract

This House rules over someone's health, debt, labor and work, routines, coworkers, maternal aunts, and uncles, as well as fear. It is able to show disease and how well one recovers from it as well as dieting habits. It will also be connected to the working and services that are provided to the individual. Additionally, it will show debt, animal relationships, hygiene, and more.

Sun in Sixth House

This shows that health is good. The individual will be defended well against illness and is likely to also be a hard worker. They respect their superiors and are willing to take the necessary precautions to keep themselves safe.

Moon in Sixth House

This position shows that the individual is likely to pay a major focus to attention to detail that can be a major benefit. They tend to focus on their natural capacity to handle people and will typically make major progress in their work because of their focus. The Moon may be afflicted here, at which point, physical weakness may occur.

Mercury in Sixth House

Mercury, in this position, typically leads to an increase in nervous disorders or anxiety. Typically the individual will have to be extremely careful with their pursuit of studies because they tend to overdo what they are doing in life. They may create restlessness, and this can hurt them at work. In retrograde, the individual will likely find that they approach the world analytically and with self-criticism. They must mature and learn to tolerate and love themselves.

Venus in Sixth House

This is largely helpful but also associated with blood disorders or diabetes. However, for work, it is quite favorable and shows that the individual will cooperate and work well with others. They prefer routine more than anything else and will appreciate serving others. However, they may suffer from sexual diseases as well. When Venus is in retrograde, they may need to ensure that feelings are carefully regulated and to work to avoid clinging to perfection.

Mars in Sixth House

Mars tends to be associated with a tendency to fevers, accidents, or suffering from dangers when work is done. However, they are capable of working quite hard. They may struggle financially after illness or accident, and they may also struggle as an employee. In retrograde, these individuals must be cautious about their health and make sure they manage their relationships with others well.

Jupiter in Sixth House

This position tends to show benefits in health, work, and employees (if applicable). Typically, these people recover well from any illnesses that they have. At work, they tend to perform well and find that they are willing to aid others if necessary. In retrograde, this person must make sure they don't focus so much on the minutia and instead focus on the wider picture. They need to find a balance between perfection and practical reality.

Saturn in Sixth House

Saturn in this position shows a tendency for colds and accidents with things falling. They may also struggle in their workplace and suffer from anxiety. This position is often connected to weaken healing capacity. Additionally, they may struggle to find employment. IN retrograde, this person tends to be excellent in organizing and dilemma solving.

Rahu in Sixth House

This is typically associated with good healing powers, and health is usually maintained through fasting. Typically, there are areas in life that need to be worked on, such as careers.

Ketu in Sixth House

This position is typically associated with a need to overcome negativity. Negativity brings disease and must be defeated. These people find peace through happiness and clearing out their karmic debts in the process. They usually look for truth and wisdom in the world.

SEVENTH HOUSE: DESCENDANT (*YUVATI BHAVA*)

Significator: Venus

Zodiac: Libra

Body parts: Kidneys, middle and lower back

This House is related to relationships, marriages, lawsuits, divorce, and enemies. Typically, this will rule all people that the individual that will be interacted with. It is referred to as the "house of union," referring to marriage. Additionally, however, it rules business partners as well.

Sun in Seventh House

This position is found to be highly beneficial to emotional development and tends to imply good marriage as well. However, they must be mindful of their differences socially or ethnically to other people. They have the potential to move up in life greatly, but they must be patient and accepting of differences to do so.

Moon in Seventh House

This tends to imply that there will be peace domestically. The partner of the individual is also likely to be highly skilled in handling family life. However, this can be the opposite of the truth if the Moon is aspected poorly. They must recognize their own attachments and how those influence them.

Mercury in Seventh House

This tends to imply the intense mental capabilities of one's partner; it is great for good, favorable relationships with in-laws. Additionally, it indicates marriage will involve travel. The individual tends to be cheery and inclined toward literary pursuits. In retrograde, however, the individual must be able to establish good judgment and motives for their relationships.

Venus in Seventh House

This is a great position for marriage. It implies that love and attraction will remain strong and that the individual will be in a good position to cooperate and help others. It indicates social and public success, along with adaptability. Marriage and finances will likely be secure. In retrograde, the individual may struggle with sensitivity.

Mars in Seventh House

This tends to imply that the native must learn to adapt to their partner's strength without being used. The partner will likely have anger issues and struggle greatly. Typically, this is translated to aggressiveness toward or from partners and can lead to problems. In retrograde, there are problems with violence and selfishness.

Jupiter in Seventh House

This is a highly favorable position that tends to imply a strong relationship. The marriage may be biracial or could show that the individual will be authoritative. The partner will be in more of a support role. This tends to translate to popularity and happy marriage. In retrograde, this individual tends to spend time dwelling non how he or she is seen by others.

Saturn in Seventh House

Saturn tends to show that the native may marry someone older, and there may be delays in the consummation of the marriage. The marriage partner tends to be frugal and cautious with spending. Additionally, the health of the partner can cause anxiety, and the partner will become problematic. This tends to cause problems to the partner, and problems with the relationship in general. In retrograde, it shows that the individual feels limited by partners and must be able to establish a connection to overcome this.

Rahu in Seventh House

This tends to imply that marriage matters immensely. Typically, the partner is more mature than the individual. Success and pleasure are only obtained through contact with the public. They are usually quite charming, but problems could arise if there is a negative aspect. This tends to put Ketu in the Ascendant, which is bad for health.

Ketu in Seventh House

Ketu in this position causes an individual to have to learn to be independent. They must take control and choose their own approaches to the world around them.

EIGHTH HOUSE (*RANDHRA BHAVA*)

Significator: Mars

Zodiac: Scorpio

Body parts: Prostate gland, reproductive system, colon

This House is in control of longevity, as well as many negatives in life. It controls defeat and sorrow while also revealing information about scandals or obstacles that must be overcome. However, it also controls sexuality, regeneration, and unearned money. Additionally, it can reveal information about death, as well. It controls the lifespan of an individual and typically will control the cause of death. It focuses strongly on misfortune and anxiety, so it is often seen as negative in general.

Sun in Eighth House

This tends to show that death will be quick, typically from heart failure. It also shows the potential to benefit through inheritance, as well as shows that partners should be capable of handling finances.

Moon in Eighth House

This shows that the most likely cause of death will be a problem with the body failing to function. However, it will likely be relatively peaceful. Additionally, there will be financial gains through legacy or unexpected gifts. They may find that they benefit from marriage or business partners, and they will typically give an inheritance as well.

Mercury in Eighth House

This indicates a problem with nervous or respiratory systems to cause death. It may be related to travel, and it could cause the individual to come into contact with conditions associated with other people dying. They may work in a job where they must work with dead bodies, for example.

Venus in Eighth House

Venus in Eighth tends to show a peaceful, natural death, possibly in sleep. It could be related to the kidneys or the throat, or it could be something else. Typically, there is an increased prospect for gain through a legacy in this position.

Mars in Eighth House

Mars here tends to be associated with sudden or violent death, such as during an operation or due to an injury. It could also be related to a fever. Typically, there are many problems for both marriage and business partners here—they may suffer from severe financial loss. There may be disputes over money as well.

Jupiter in Eighth House

This is typically deemed to be a favorable position, and death is typically from natural causes. The individual will usually leave behind a legacy and may also find that their partner I naturally skilled with money, meaning that financial worries will not be as big of a deal. They may gain through the death of friends or family, and in the eighth House, they may have big inheritances. When Jupiter is in retrograde, the individual tends to have a good sense of other people's values. They will attempt to transform others, require their own independence, and will seek out knowledge.

Saturn in Eighth House

When Saturn is in the Eighth House, the individual is likely to have bad health. This can cause problems with prolonging conditions that will cause death, meaning that the individual is likely to suffer. Additionally, it reveals that there are chronic ailments that will have to be endured. Senility may begin to develop earlier than normal, or they may find that they suffer in other ways. There may be other ways that they end up suffering. They may struggle with their marriage or business, and this can be a problem. This placement of Saturn implies that there will be a violent death, no support financially from others, and general suffering. However, in retrograde, this can add limitations to sexuality as well. On the plus side, there may be some talent at work.

Rahu in Eighth House

In this position, the individual must learn to welcome and accept the help that other people offer financially. You will find that money is primarily obtained through other partners, and though this can be difficult to take, you must be able to welcome that humility and recognize that life is connected. If afflicted, this sign can lead to problems with poverty or financial losses.

Ketu in Eighth House

In this position, you may realize that you've got a need to develop your personal resources, whether they are talents, passions, money, possessions, or anything else, so that they can be shared in a partnership. You must be able to recognize that you can share with other people and see that connection. Partners must share, and that can be difficult for you if you are under this sign.

NINTH HOUSE (*DHARMA BHAVA*)

Significator: *Jupiter*

Zodiac: *Sagittarius*

Body parts: *thighs hips, buttocks*

This House is responsible for knowledge, education, teaching, longer journeys, luck, grandchildren, and more. It can also be highly tied to religion and philosophy as well, along with faith and worship. Typically, this House will determine how religious someone will be, and it will also show fortunes that are resultant of the past lives that someone may have had. They will also show how much knowledge has been gained as well. This is a highly important sign that will require you to look closer at it to understand just how you will get through life.

Sun in Ninth House

This is a good position for the sun. For women, it implies that they may marry someone that is foreign or someone that has been met during travels. Additionally, it can enhance the opportunities for progress, dignity, and prestige. It can show that the individual is likely to be attracted to the idea of religion and the peace it brings with it, along with ceremonies.

Moon in Ninth House

In this position, the Moon influences the individual to desire to travel regularly. They may find that they are the most successful financially and socially when they are traveling abroad, and they may even choose to live in another country altogether. Typically, this is intensified by water or air signs. These people tend to be conservative with their religions and may also be highly imaginative and open-minded with plenty of interest in philosophy and metaphysics. They may also find that they enjoy traveling plenty and meeting new people.

Mercury in Ninth House

This position is decent for Mercury. Usually, it shows that thoughts and inspirational powers are highly accentuated. Typically, these people will be optimistic, but it can also lend itself to restlessness and confusion at times. These people are keenly interested in law, philosophy, and religion. Typically, they pursue learning foreign languages to better communicate out of their home country. In retrograde, the individual may find that they need to question themselves and their tolerance toward others more. They need to make sure that they are not overthinking things.

Venus in Ninth House

This position leads to people who are highly philosophical by nature. They are cheerful and optimistic as well, thanks to Venus's influence. They are typically quite spiritual and prefer to travel as well, but they are also focused more on being comfortable than experiencing new things. They are typically willing to follow a single religion and typically find that they are quite good with the relatives of those around them. In retrograde, the individual will find that they have a high drive for freedom.

Mars in Ninth House

In this position, Mars can indicate an attraction to traveling, especially if it is adventurous. However, this usually brings danger to it, and you will need to weight this to determine if it is worthwhile. Typically, these people tend to be highly defensive of their religions and will typically do anything to defend them. They may grow angry and aggressive, which needs to be cooled and tamed to avoid problems. Their rigidity can be problematic for them, and they may find that they are almost fanatical at times. In retrograde, these people need to find their freedom and may find that they are driven by their religions.

Jupiter in Ninth House

This House is known for making the native quite successful financially. This success and financial security will likely come from overseas ventures. Typically, they may find that they are highly religious and may even be in highly important religious positions. They are typically attracted to the fanfare of the ceremony. In retrograde, this person is typically free-minded and dislikes the idea of getting married.

Saturn in Ninth House

Saturn in this position can create strong opinions of religion as well as an interest in the occult in life. It can also create financial success overseas, depending upon the influence. However, the individual should not travel away for too long. There is great depth philosophically here, but there could be issues with long journeys. In retrograde, this can create a wise individual, though they may doubt themselves. Their spiritual journey typically concludes with them finally locating their self-worth.

Rahu in Ninth House

This can cause problems for people that are not spiritually developed. They may need to learn to begin to communicate their issues. Typically, they disregard the idea of religion under this sign, and that can cause them problems. Usually, they will find themselves working with some sort of foreign affairs at some point through a coincidence somewhere along the way.

Ketu in Ninth House

This position is typically recognized by creating a need to know. The individual is highly driven by their need for knowledge from the world around them and any problems that may be encountered. They want to address everything with logic, and while they may have been religious in the past, they are not really religious any longer. They usually see that there is no one religion that is *the* religion, and as such, they tend to look at the world around them through the eyes of someone interested in understanding what is going on around them.

TENTH HOUSE (*KARMA BHAVA*)

Significator: *Saturn and Mars*

Zodiac: *Capricorn*

Body parts: *Gallbladder and knees*

This House is highly influential over one's work and economic standing and success. Effectively, if it is related to your name, your honor, your recognition, or fame, it is ruled by the Tenth House. This means that you will want to look to this to identify everything that you will become. It is the apex of your horoscope—it shows you exactly what you will become in terms of your success and the people around you.

Sun in Tenth House

This position shows that the Sun will radiate outward, creating a position in which the native is able to run their own business. When you look at this, you will see that someone will have high levels of prestige and reputation, both of which will be attained by the native. This allows for better character development and allows them to work in a tremendous capacity as a leader and organizer. They can make great headway and become highly successful. For best results, he must be able to coordinate with the opportunities of those around him.

Moon in Tenth House

In this position, the Moon influences advancement both politically and publically. This individual will likely find their life filled with opportunities to travel and explore the world. They are highly influential, and the Moon will bring success in daily life, along with financial success as well. There is evidence that there will be a peaceful home life as well.

Mercury in Tenth House

When Mercury is in the Tenth House, you see that the individual should find success in an admin or executive position. This will happen regardless of the field, and especially in a field such as journalism. Mercury will create excellent clerical and secretarial success. The individual is likely to behave quite straightforwardly and, as a result, is likely to find success with efficiency. They are likely to be honest, and that brings success. In retrograde, this can cause a need to impress other people.

Venus in Tenth House

Venus, in this position, tends to create a drive to be involved in artistic professions. These are typically singing, acting, or dancing and the native tends to find great success one way or another in these positions. Additionally, they find that they are driven by their need to succeed in banking or insurance. You may see that these people are skilled at blending politics with personal life, and as a result, they are able to get great levels of prestige. In retrograde, this can cause a high level of sensitivity for social values, along with creative acuity.

Mars in Tenth House

Mars, in this position, tends to imply that the individual's professional life is based in either architecture or engineering. This individual may find that they choose to go into some sort of STEM field, and they will find that their spirit to achieve is bolstered. However, they must be mindful that they avoid risks that are not needed—those can cause problems. Additionally, these people must make sure that they avoid giving in to their impulses. These people tend to be driven strongly toward success. In retrograde, these people tend to dwell too much on their careers.

Jupiter in Tenth House

This position for Jupiter is highly favorable for the career life. This individual is likely to pursue legal fields and may be inspired to pursue a career as a lawyer or a judge. Additionally, they are likely to find the best financial success overseas. They tend to be highly talented and also able to use their social position to their advantage. Even if they never pursue law, they will find that they focus on the world with that legal understanding of things. Jupiter in this House tends to imply success in careers. In retrograde, this can cause the individual to focus on getting approval from others while also trying to establish their own freedom.

Saturn in Tenth House

Saturn in this position tends to show high levels of influence over the individual, and this will depend upon the aspect to determine if it is good or bad. With a good aspect, the individual will be highly successful in business, profession, and social life. However, with a bad aspect, it can cause strife throughout life. The individual is likely to find that they are constantly involved with the commercial side of life, and they will find that they must indicate that they are capable of adjusting their expectations to ensure that they are happy. They will have a to of work in life, but if they learn to manage it, they can find that they are highly successful. In retrograde, this person is likely to be highly conscientious and responsible as a direct result. They are likely to attempt to be principled.

Rahu in Tenth House

In this position, Rahu implies success in the career, but it will be checkered. Sometimes, they will succeed, but they will find that for their success, they must sacrifice their home life to begin to get that better public life as well. They will find themselves the recipients of honor and recognition. However, they have probably struggled with their parents and, as a result, struggle. Their first half of life is far less enjoyable than the first.

Ketu in Tenth House

When Ketu is in the Tenth House, the individual feels a need to find emotional stability and peace based on domestics. They will work to control their emotions to build that stability if necessary, and they tend to concentrate on their souls over their egos. However, if they are not focused enough, they may find that they look for social benefits instead. '

ELEVENTH HOUSE *(LABHA BHAVA)*

Significator: *Sun*

Zodiac: *Aquarius*

Body parts: *Ankles, calves*

This House is focused on one's social circles, profits, income, and desire, as well as whether wishes are fulfilled. You will be able to tell a lot about ht friends that you have based upon this House. You will also be able to identify the success that the individual is likely to have, as well as relationships with the elder brother or sister and the paternal uncle

Sun in Eleventh House

This is a great position for the Sun—it shows that the individual is going to have friends in highly influential places, and those friends will be able to aid the individual plenty in their life with any plans that they have. The friends may even be able to aid with finances if necessary. It is highly favorable for both social and public actions, and they should be able to strike a good balance between social life and professional success.

Moon in Eleventh House

This position shows a large capacity for good friendships that last. Additionally, it shows that those friends will be likely to be beneficial over time. They are able to be connected to the individual's domestic life. This individual is likely to find themselves attached to social or welfare work. Through this, they are able to make friends by making them feel at ease while they work. This individual is skilled at talking and encouraging cooperation with other people. This creates a happy, friendly individual with visionary tendencies.

Mercury in Eleventh House

With Mercury in this position, the individual is likely to find friendships through knowledge-based means, typically through education or intellectual pursuits. The individual is probably quite serious and works to cooperate intellectually with other people. They are attracted to science and experiments and will be skilled in social and public life more so than professional. Typically, they will be able to bring harmony to friends, neighbors, and family. The circle of friends is likely based upon intellectual pursuits and beliefs more than anything else. In retrograde, this can cause a need for novelty and new experience.

Venus in Eleventh House

In this position, the individual is likely to find that their friendships and associations with people are strong and secure. Venus will up the affections that the individual has, and it is also likely that many friends are likely women, with many connected to artistic purposes in life. The individual must be cautious with how much money is spent on entertainment or other frivolous things, but they will find that they naturally draw people who need advice. Typically, they are willing to provide endless advice, and their friendships rapidly become romantic in nature. In retrograde, this can create curiosity as well as distance in relationships.

Mars in Eleventh House

This indicates a likelihood that the individual is going to create friendships rapidly, though they may be impulsive and unwise at times. They may find themselves in a bad position with people they thought were friends. Most of these friends will be men, and the individual must be mindful to avoid impulsiveness to make sure that those around them are actually good friends. In retrograde, this individual will spend plenty of energy in their dreams, but may not manage to manifest them if not careful with how they go about it.

Jupiter in Eleventh House

In this position, the individual is likely to find that they have great, long-lasting friendships that will aid them in ensuring that they are successful in life. These friends will be important, materially, and spiritually as well. The individual is likely to find that their wishes are achieved through gaining the support from these friends that are made over time. These people will find that they are able to build up that support carefully, and as a result, they will be highly successful. In retrograde, they are likely to be driven by curiosity and a desire for something new. They want to learn as much as they possibly can in life.

Saturn in Eleventh House

This placement for Saturn shows a struggle in friendships. Those with this placement tend to struggle most with trying to figure out how to connect. They may be shy or struggle to get along with other people. When they make friendships, however, those friendships are highly enduring. That is beneficial to them, and the people that they befriend tend to be older than the individual. This placement is often tied to unpopularity, struggling to plan, not getting what one wishes for the most. In retrograde, they can find that they are a dreamer that will be able to achieve that success through patience and careful attention to detail.

Rahu in Eleventh House

This position shows that someone makes friends that are in a better position from the individual; they are then able to aid the individual closely. They are able to become humanitarian as they begin to realize their dreams. However, they may struggle with their relationships and romantic interests, and as a result, they end up unhappy often. Additionally, they can struggle with children.

Ketu in Eleventh House

This position is connected to a need to reveal their creativity to those around them, by looking to their children or friends. They typically find that their friends worked for them in the past, and now, they are dependent upon their friends. They must learn to develop their own creativity to benefit their friends as well to create common benefits amongst each other.

TWELFTH HOUSE (VAIRAGYA BHAVA)

Significator: Saturn

Zodiac: Pisces

Body parts: Feet

This House is typically related to one's confinement or bondage in life. It is indicative of poverty, suffering, misery, phobias, and final emancipation from the cycle of birth and death. It effectively shows limitations but also escaping the situation entirely. This House is highly related to being able to make problems for the individual. However, it can also influence charity, donations, and investments as well. It will also show unselfishness and sacrifice.

Sun in Twelfth House

The Sun in this position typically implies that at least one-third of the individual's life will be filled with misfortune. This could determine whether the individual can escape from that misfortune or if he or she will allow for those misfortunes to take over everything. It is highly dependent upon the aspects. Typically, these individuals will find that they lean toward psychic exploration.

Moon in Twelfth House

With the Moon in this position, the individual is likely to be met with restriction and limitation. It is perfect if you want to be a monk, nun, or a nurse or doctor, thanks to the fact that it emphasizes those in charity or sympathy work. The individual is likely to be carrying their own secrets or carrying the secrets of other people instead. They may find that they are indiscreet in love affairs, allowing their enjoyment to take control rather than carrying about practicality. Additionally, this individual is likely to emphasize living life internally, focusing inwardly, and living an introverted life. They are likely to find problems with their mother and may struggle in their professions.

Mercury in Twelfth House

This position shows that the individual has a subtle mind. They may find that risks are worth it and may also choose to get out and pursue danger every now and then. When well aspected, they tend to show a focus on the occult. Additionally, they may focus on mysteries or working through these trains of thought. Typically, they are skilled with imagination and being able to visualize. They can also create enemies relatively easily by criticizing others. When in retrograde, they may find that they are inwardly turned, focusing on their own spirituality. Additionally, they may find that they are highly talented with music or metaphysics.

Venus in Twelfth House

This creates an inclination toward romance and even an early marriage, though they will find that they may struggle sometimes. They find that they are able to enjoy secret happiness, but also suffer in secret silence as well. They may find that their affections are one of the biggest problems in their lives. They may struggle in their romantic life. In retrograde, they often find that they struggle with emotions that cannot be shown to others. Additionally, it shows creativity, but without willing to be forced into it. They want to find their own fulfillment but also don't want to get attached to their past as well.

Mars in Twelfth House

Mars shows that this individual is likely to struggle through life and misfortune. They are likely to behave impulsively rather than rationally, and this can cause problems. This individual may find themselves imprisoned falsely, suffering from misplacing their affections, or suffering injuries afflicted by an enemy. It can create a lifelong struggle with finances and live in poverty. It could also show that the individual may get involved in war and find themselves imprisoned. This can cause problems for the subconscious. In retrograde, this requires you to become constructive with energy to prevent feeling trapped. There is an emphasis on the lesson to forgive and forget.

Jupiter in Twelfth House

This position typically implies that at least one-third of the individual's life will suffer from misfortune. Additionally, they will find that they are caught up in their own troubles regularly often. They must build up their skills to be able to remove themselves from the dwelling so that they can find success. However, you will probably find that you are benevolent and interested in having a positive outlook toward the future. You will likely be lucky because Jupiter will protect you, helping you to come out on top and to preserve your generous soul, even when you do suffer.

Saturn in Twelfth House

Saturn in this position tends to create feelings of restriction and unhappiness in their life as well as drawing bad luck. Typically, this shows that someone is quite independent and prefers being alone. It is unfavorable for all but those who do enjoy the peace and quiet of this time to themselves. Typically, this person may end up hospitalized or imprisoned in some other way. There will be hardship brought into life thanks to this position. In retrograde, the individual will likely become highly introspective. They will find that they focus intently on truth, success, and maturity.

Rahu in Twelfth House

This implies that an individual must learn plenty about their lives and they must learn about self-sacrifice. They must learn to help other people to be able to succeed.

Ketu in Twelfth House

This shows a need to improve relations with someone else based on their services. They usually find that they make an effort to take routine responsibilities. Typically, they find themselves isolated somehow, whether in prison, personally as a recluse, or in a monastery or hospital. They tend to think mostly about themselves, though they want to help others. When they can't meet that responsibility, they may find that they choose addictions or to back out by expecting other people to care for them instead.

CHAPTER 7:
THE LUNAR MANSIONS

Remember that the myth of the Moon that was discussed earlier in the book told of the Moon had twenty-seven wives that were all sisters. He had his preference for Rohini but was forced to spend time with all of them after his father-in-law, hearing the pleas of his other daughters, cursed him with consumption that caused him to begin to wane away. As a result, other gods feared that life would be altered on Earth and appealed to Daksha, father of the Moon's wives, to change the curse. Instead, the Moon was cursed to spend time with each daughter one day per month, waning in power for fourteen days and gaining power for fourteen days as well, leaving just one day each month without a Moon.

The ancient Indians looked up to the sky and referred to these as Lunar Mansions—the Nakshatras—that helped to divide up the sky. This was the initial form of astrology that can even be found referenced up to 10,000 years ago. To identify which Lunar Mansion your Moon was in at birth will help you know more about yourself, what drives you, and more. If you know what your position is in Western charts, all you have to do is subtract 23 from it, and you will have your answer.

Knowing what your Nakshatra is will help you to begin to understand more about yourself. It is necessary for you to get the fullest picture of yourself, your own birth chart, and everything else. Thankfully, you won't have to go back and hunt down the Moon's position upon your birth—any Vedic astrology birth chart calculator should give this to you without a problem.

ASWINI: THE HORSE GODDES

00 degrees 00' –13 degrees 20' Aries

If you were born under this Lunar Mansion, you will desire life and even become quite restless. You will not tolerate boredom well and will find that you are constantly on the move for something new and exciting. You are quick to think and are likely to need to make sure that you do not react too hastily to avoid becoming impulsive. You may find that you are reluctant to accept responsibility and may get frustrated or even aggressive if you don't get things to go the way that you wanted. You are likely to be a natural healer.

BHARANI: THE RIVER OF SOULS

13 degrees 20' – 26 degrees 40' Aries

This is a sign that is both sensuous and artistic, but also turbulent in the passions at times. Typically, you can find that you hyper-focus on something to the point of extremity at times, and you will find that you are entirely ruled by your goals that you have set out. This sign requires you to master your emotions and find your sense of compassion. Personal transformation will be key here to help you to avoid struggles of willpower and impulsivity. This is a mystical position, and you may find that you have a tendency toward shamanic or mystic information.

KRITTICA: THE STAR OF FIRE

26 degrees 40' Aries – 10' Taurus

This is typically intensely emotional. You can find yourself driven by radical beliefs and desiring truth no matter what. However, you must be mindful of the fact that your desire to speak the truth at all costs can inflict pain on other people, and you will have to cope with this. You must learn to find tact to tame your tongue. Additionally, you can find that you are self-motivated and proud, something powerful if you can control the impulsive nature that you have. You are just as witty as you are sharp, and that can help you immensely.

ROHINI: THE RED GODDESS

10 degrees 23'—23 degrees 20' Taurus

This was the Moon's favorite wife and is an erotic goddess. When you are born here, you may find that you are attractive, charming, and focus on artistic ventures. You are romantic and seek culture to enjoy. You value honesty and being able to communicate well, while also being true to your beliefs that you have. However, you likely also have a philosophical side to you that you must balance with that need for luxury. You must be cautious to avoid falling for your material desires.

MRIGASHIRA: THE STAR OF SEARCHING

23 degrees 20' Taurus – 06 degrees 40' Gemini

This star will show you a life that is passionate and without need for rest. You are powerful, and you will always be pursuing something. You are always seeking out more knowledge, and you are great at communicating as well, meaning that you may find your place in speaking and writing. However, when you struggle with your nature, you can end up with firm views in life that must be managed. You might end up being a bit moody at times, and while you are gentle in nature, it can be tough to avoid temptation at times, and you could find yourself overindulging somewhat regularly.

ARDRA: THE TEAR DROP

05 degrees 40' – 20 degrees 00' Gemini

This sign is commonly associated with the storm god, Rudra. When you were born under this sign, you can find that your emotions are as unpredictable as the storms, and you can find that you feel passionately and deeply, emphasizing the mind and your ability to think. When you are born under this sign, you will find that you are able to gain great rewards in life, but only if you can persist.

PUNAVASU: THE LIGHT BRINGER

20 degrees 00' Gemini – 03 degrees 20' Cancer

This is the calm after the storm of Ardra. It creates an individual that is kind, friendly, agreeable, and adaptive with an emphasis on looking at the philosophical side of things. You will tend to be on the sensitive side, appreciating, and enjoying the arts. You will enjoy your home life but also find that you enjoy traveling. You find that you want to make sure that everyone is happy at all times, and that causes major problems for you.

PUSHYA: NOURISHMENT

03 degrees 20' – 16 degrees 40' Cancer

This tends to be a sign that you've got the support that you need. You will also have the makings of someone that is supportive of others, making you a great, mature friend that people can turn to. You know how to manage your own emotions so that they cannot completely overwhelm you. You use this wisdom to keep yourself working toward the goals that you care for.

ASHLESHA: THE COILED SERPENT

16 degrees 40' – 30 degrees 00' Cancer

This sign gives you the ability to gain a real sense of wisdom from taking a close look at the darkest reaches of your soul. You tend to be philosophical in nature and typically find that your mind is eager to penetrate everything. You want to be independent but are also a bit reclusive. You tend to be very sensuous, and along with that, you are quite intuitive as well, meaning that you can pass very accurate judgments on others just with your own gut feelings.

MAGHA: THE FOREFATHERS

00 degrees 00' – 13 degrees 20' Leo

This is a great sign for being born under—you will be proud, but conservative, and you will be able to follow the paths of the ancestors. You will be big-hearted, sensuous, but still deeply passionate about the world that you are in. You will find that you must be mindful of power or wealth, or you can become snobbish in nature. However, you have the power to be a great individual, one that is highly beneficial and worth pursuing.

PURVA PHALGUNI: THE WORLD TREE GODDESS

13 degrees 20' – 26 degrees 40' Leo

This is a sign of romance, love, and partnership. If you are under this sign, you are likely to emphasize those romantic relationships in your life above all else, and you will have that attitude of a romantic to go with it. You are likely to be highly affectionate, passionate, and love life around you. You will have good luck as a result of this attitude, and as a result, you will find that you are quite happy in life. However, you must be mindful not to overindulge, which can cause narcissism.

UTTARA PHALGUNI: THE MARRIAGE GODDESS

26 degrees 40' Leo—10 degrees 00 Virgo'

You are someone who is attracted to love and relationships, and they are a source of happiness for you. You may also find that you will take it further, finding a growing interest in tantra or mysticism surrounding sex. Your personality is highly attractive, and you are kind, willing to give, and compassionate, so others see you as a source of comfort and compassion. You want to help others to prevent suffering. However, you must make sure that your desire to be in a relationship does not make you stay in one that is restrictive to your ability to grow.

HASTA: SKILLED ACTIVITIES

10 degrees 00'—23 degrees 00' Virgo

This sign will create a complex individual that is industrious and hard-working, yet creative and intelligent at the same time. You are incredibly intelligent and talented, but you also tend to flip flop back and forth, making it difficult for you to make meaningful decisions in life. You must make sure that you are caring and supportive, and that you are able to explore your talents in the world.

CHITRA: THE JEWEL

23 degrees 20' Virgo – 06 degrees 40' Libra

This sign is as shiny as the jewel it was named after. Your mind is radiant, elegant, and charismatic, and you are constantly seeking to polish it. You want to make sure that you can be original, and yet, you also want to balance your thinking and analysis at the same time. You tend to focus on that natural flair that you have, and you find it hard to believe that other people don't have the talent and creative skill that you do. You are stuck trying to find a way to prevent overindulgence.

SWATI: THE WIND GOD

06 degrees 40' – 20 degrees 00' Libra

This sign is highly flexible and independent at the same time. However, it is as restless, light, and flexible as the wind. It can bend and bow as much as necessary, but that flexibility leads to indecision. You will naturally love art, learning, and literature, and you will be able to manage businesses as well. You are similar to Chitra, but at the same time, you are more generous and charitable. However, the restlessness can lead to being scattered. Additionally, you will also need some time to relax and sometimes unwind as well.

VISHAKHA: THE MOON OF POWER

20 degrees 00' Libra – 03 degrees 20' Scorpio

This sign creates people brimming with ambition and competitive nature, paired with the necessary tenacity to make their goals actually happen. However, they must take care not to be too obsessive at times, and they will need to find a way to balance their desires with what needs to be done to prevent burnout from constantly moving on the go. You must make sure that you have the ability to research and acquire the knowledge that exists around you. You can be quite patient and fortuitous if you can work on yourself.

ANURADHA: THE MOON OF FRIENDSHIP

03 degrees 20' – 16 degrees 40' Scorpio

These people are those that are cooperative in nearly all areas of their lives, friendly and happy to engage with others. They tend to be great lovers as well, gentle but still bravely passionate at the same time. When you are born under this sign, you tend to be organized and enjoy traveling. You will likely find that you are the most successful when you are far away from your birthplace. However, you are highly sensitive and likely have little tolerance for other people's frustration or your own, and as a result, you find that you can't control your emotions.

JYESHTHA: THE WISDOM CRONE

16 degrees 40' – 30 degrees 00' Scorpio

This creates crafty, analytical, and skillful people that are capable of subtleties. You are likely magical and even enigmatic at times, but your soul is also quite tumultuous. You may find that you have a strong personality, but that can become either arrogant or reclusive, depending upon how it manifests itself. Additionally, you will find that you constantly search for your knowledge from those around you, looking to the darkest places to find and use that wisdom for yourself. You can gain it through all sorts of experiences to allow yourself to become a provider.

MULA: THE ROOT OF ALL THINGS

30 degrees 00' – 13 degrees 20' Sagittarius

This sign is associated with philosophers and inquisitive individuals. You will find that you enjoy diving deeply into just about anything that you read, and you will constantly seek time to persist in your attempts to gain knowledge about the world around you. You are passionate about what you love and find that you are powerful and even bold in terms of your personality. You will strive forward with no regard for stopping when you have your mindset on something. However, you may also find that you feel sometimes trapped when circumstances are not favorable for you.

PURVA ASHADHA: THE MOON OF EARLY VICTORY

13 degrees 20' – 26 degrees 40' Sagittarius

This sign shows success early on in life. You will develop into a proud individual with an almost invincible attitude, feeling like you will never back down. You will argue endlessly and fervently, and you find that you usually actually do have that necessary power over other people. However, you find that you still have the emotional depth to you, and you are willing to share it with people that you care for. You are strongly intuitive and empathetic, and you use this to your advantage to help soften your edges a bit. You tend to focus on the philosophy and spiritual aspects of your life to get through the tough times.

UTTARA ASHADHA: THE MOON OF LATER VICTORY

26 degrees 40' Sagittarius – 10 degrees 00' Capricorn

This sign influences people into idealistic individuals—people who are dedicated to being humanitarian and idealistic in value. They tend to be strongly committed to the goals that they set and work hard with high ambitions to ensure that they can build up that sense of responsibility that they have. Typically, you find that you are capable of delving into your own mind well, and you will succeed more later in life when you've found a way to valance out your need for enthusiastically identifying what drives you with that restlessness that tends to keep you down. You will need to make sure that your achievements are somewhat permanent so that you will be able to complete everything that you need to do. You will be able to form good friendships through doing so, and in the process, you will communicate well.

SHRAVANA: THE MOON OF LISTENING

10 degrees 00' – 23 degrees 20' Capricorn

If you were born in this sign, you will find that you prefer to work through oral traditions more than anything else. You focus on the traditional in just about any aspect in life, and you will find that you are highly serious and dedicated to anything that you study. You will constantly hunger to learn something new, and you will work hard to satiate it in any way that you can. Additionally, you are probably sensitive, and you may find that you struggle early on in life, but find success later on.

DANISHTHA: THE DRUMMER

23 degrees 20' Capricorn – 06 degrees 40' Aquarius

This sign creates people who are optimistically liberal—they are ambitious and willing to work hard to create the world that they want to see, but are also powerfully motivated as well. These people are able to create the changes in the world that they want to see and are oftentimes happiest in control of the change and life that they want to see in their life. However, they also require space away from home, and they need to ensure that they do not allow their need for power and control to cause them to become cruel or disregard what other people also need. They must be able to balance that patience with their drive for ambition and success.

SHATABHISHA: THE DIVINE HEALER

06 degrees 40' – 20 degrees 00' Aquarius

Those born under this sign tend to be reclusive—they prefer to be on their own—and they are fiercely independent as well. Typically quite mystical in nature, they will typically bury their heads in learning about the world around them. Philosophy, science, psychology, and metaphysics are all topics that are endlessly fascinating to these people. Typically, you will find that these people will choose to be on their own, focusing on the world of their studies rather than connecting to other people. Additionally, these people tend to favor making big changes in their lives—when they struggle under a crisis, they can find ways to overcome it.

PURVA BHADRAPADA: THE FIRE DRAGON

20 degrees 00' Aquarius – 03 degrees 20' Pisces

This is the sign of transforming, removing, and discarding the old to be able to create the new. You tend to be highly passionate and will spread that passion through your words, becoming great at speaking and communicating. You are highly driven and will focus your eyes on what you care about the most: Your own social reform plan that you would like to see achieved. Additionally, you are likely to be eccentric at times, but also strong and determined as well. You might see that the world around you is not really kind, and you may find yourself to be suspicious and untrusting because of this, but you will also work hard to transform the world around you into something that is kinder.

UTTARA BHADRAPADA: THE DRAGON OF THE DEEP

03 degrees 20' – 16 degrees 40' Pisces

This sign creates people who are highly communicative—you will be able to speak and write with skill and grace that is both restrained in how it presents to other people but also is highly passionate as well. You can tow that line well with clarity and insight, and you can ensure that you create those compelling speeches to motivate people toward your cause. You will need to take time to yourself sometimes, and you will tend to use your intuition to the best of your ability.

REVATI: THE MOON OF SPLENDOR

16 degrees 40' – 30 degrees 00 Pisces

This sign is highly nurturing. These individuals will find themselves to be responsible and humanitarian in value. They tend to care for those that need it the most and are always happy to help other people when they need it the most. These people are naturally quite generous and find that they always have a way of getting everything that they need, whether they pursue it or not. They are able to enjoy a softer touch, kind and sensitive to those around them, and choose to create rather than hurt. These people may be disappointed early on and feel that the world is harsh, but instead of using that truth to harden themselves, they choose to help others instead, to discover that balance. They prefer to help other people become the people that they were destined to be through any means possible.

CHAPTER 8:
THE SIGNIFICANCE OF VEDIC ASTROLOG

Vedic astrology, no doubt, has plenty of significance for a major amount of the population. In India, it is commonly utilized on a regular basis, allowing for the understanding of life and the things that we may not have an understanding of. Vedic astrology offers that option to begin to understand the difference between what is going on externally and internally. It allows for an understanding of past lives and what may have happened to create current situations. It is one of those aspects of life that will highly aid in being able to plan one's own life.

So many people around the world look to Vedic astrology when it comes to their major decisions in life. From being able to name children to look at marriage compatibility or anything else, many people wholeheartedly rely on Vedic astrology to help them to make the best possible choices for themselves. They count on the stars, with all of their wisdom and information that they hold, to reveal everything they need to know in life. They are able to know what they believe that the world has in store for them, and as a direct result, they then begin to better approach their lives, informed and ready to take appropriate action. Think about it—you gain so much information from looking at your birth chart, and we've spent the bulk of this book just learning to decipher that information. This is information that can be life-changing—if you understand what you are likely to suffer from, you can then begin to take precautions. If you know that life is likely to test you in certain ways, you will be able to act accordingly to protect yourself. This is essential—it helps you to be certain that you are living to your best, fullest extent. Within this chapter, we are going to take some time to identify just how significant that Vedic astrology can be in life, emphasizing just some of the ways that people today look to the stars to dictate their lives.

VEDIC ASTROLOGY AND NAMING CHILDREN

The name that you give to your child is perhaps the most important gift that you give them in life. This gift is something that you provide to them to shape their future, and it is all that remains of the individual after they pass. Names must be carefully given—they must be thought about and ensured that they have the best possible meanings to grant children the best possible luck. This is done with regard to one's birth chart to determine the right letters to use for the starting of your child's name. You have a few options for doing so. Typically, the favorite involves utilizing the Lagna—the Ascendant. When you have your Ascendant for your child, you can then pick out the letters that correlate best with your child's birth chart. For this, you will get the following:

Lagna	Letters
Aries	A, Aa, Sha
Taurus	E, Ee, Uu, Sha
Gemini	Uu, Sa
Cancer	Ga, Ea, S
Leo	O, La
Virgo	A
Libra	Ka, Ga, Da
Scorpio	Cha, Jha,
Sagittarius	Ta, Dha, Nha
Capricorn	Tha, Dha, Na
Aquarius	Pha, Bha, Ma
Pisces	Ya, Ra, La, Va

As you can see, there are plenty of options there. However, if those letters do not give you something favorable

THE SIGNIFICANCE OF VEDIC ASTROLOG| 155

when you identify the Ascendant for your child's name, you have other options as well. The second common way of choosing out a name for children based on their birth chart involves looking to the position of the Moon at birth instead, drawing from the Lunar Mansions. This then provides 27 more sets of letters that can be drawn from. These include:

Lunar Mansion	Letters
Aswini	Chu, Che, Cho, La
Bharani	Lee, Lu, Le, Lo
Krittica	A, E, U, Ea
Rohini	O, Va, Vi, Vu
Mrigashira	We, Wo, Ka, Ki
Ardra	Ku, Gha, Dha, Jha
Punavasu	Ke, Ko, Ha, Hi
Pushya	Hu, He, Ho, Da
Ashlesha	De, Du, Do
Magha	Ma, Me, Mu
Purva Phalguni	Mo, Ta, Ti, Tu
Uttara Phalguni	Te, To, Pa, Pe
Hasta	Phu, Sha, Na, Teha
Chitra	Pe, Po, Ra, Re
Swati	Ru, Re, Ro, Taa
Vishakha	Tee, Tue, Teaa, Too
Anuradha	Na, Ne, Nu
Jyeshtha	No, Ya, Yi, Uu
Mula	Ye, Yo, Ba, Be
Purva Ashadya	Bu, Dha, Ea, Eaa
Uttara Ashadya	Be, Bo, Ja, Ji
Shravana	Ju, Je, Jo, Sha
Danishtha	Ga, Gi, Gu, Ge
Shatabhisha	Go, Sa, Si, Su
Purva Bhadrapada	Se, So, Da, Di
Uttara Bhadrapada	Du
Revati	De, Do, Cha, Chi

While it is not a hard and fast rule that you must follow these conventions, it is commonly recommended so that children have a name that is fitting for one's birth chart. This is just one of the many significant ways that people turn to Vedic astrology to aid in life.

VEDIC ASTROLOGY AND KARMA

Think of your birth chart as a balance sheet—it is effectively the accumulation of karma throughout the many lives that you have had. We've already briefly touched upon Karma—the force that is created by the actions of another person. This is essential to the very life that you lead. It is simply cause and effect, and the lives that you have lived in the past have built up karma, both good and bad, over centuries of lives, actions, and decisions. Those all build upon one another to create something new that you will then need to face. This is the basis of karma itself. When you start your life, you will be reaping the fruits that your decisions in the past life have sown. Sound unfair? The truth is, you are still you, whether it is this life, last life, or five lives ago. Your soul is the same regardless of the experience as a living being. You have lessons to learn, and karma helps you to do exactly that.

The ultimate goal is to be free from the cycle of rebirth—to reach that state in which your soul has been liberated, and that requires you to be able to clear out all bad karma. There are lessons that must be learned. Karma will eventually teach you these, but whether it takes you five lifetimes or fifty to learn will be up to you and the actions that you take. Nevertheless, your horoscope will provide you with all the information that you will need to know if you want to better understand where you stand. You will be able to tell if you have a lot of karma weighing on you, or if you are well on your way to that liberation.

Karma comes in four forms, all of which have their own Houses that will provide you with information to deciphering them. These are:

- **Sanchita karma:** This shows your accumulated karma that has been sown in past lives that is mature and ready to be reaped—these are influencing your current life. These are found in the _Fourth, Eighth, and Twelfth Houses._

- **Pralabda karma**: This represents karmic transactions that are not yet completed—they were started in a previous life, and they must be dealt with in your current life. You can see these in the _Fifth House_, as well as manifested in your _First, Fifth, and Ninth Houses_ physically. These are not yet fully manifested, and you can sway them somewhat. They are represented by Rahu and Ketu. Ketu influences your karmic debt, while Rahu shows how likely you are to deal with them.

- **Kriyaman karma**: This represents the current karma that you create during your current life. This is karma, which will impact you either in the future during this life or in a future life instead. You will identify this karma through the _Third, Seventh, and Eleventh Houses_.

- **Aagmi karma**: This shows future birth karma if your current life is not your last.

As you can see, karma matters, and when you can read your horoscope, you will be able to begin understanding what the karma that you face in life really means. This is essential if you want to make sure that you are able to get through life and finally achieve your liberation. Remember, ignorance is rarely actually bliss—being informed is one of the best things that you can do. When you are informed, you can understand where you stand in the universe—you can see that karma manifested in front of yourself right there for you to read and understand. Then, you can begin to make the changes that you will need to be successful in your life.

VEDIC ASTROLOGY AND MATCHMAKING

Traditional marriage in India happens through Kundli matchmaking—which happens through Vedic astrology.

Kundli matching works to check the bride and groom to determine whether or not that couple is likely to have a happy, successful marriage. Of course, there are cases where Kundli matching has failed to accurately predict, and there have been couples who were approved with Kundli that failed to remain married. Additionally, there are times where there have been people who were deemed incompatible that were able to have long, happy marriages. However, this is a great way to begin understanding whether two people are fundamentally compatible. Remember, Vedic astrology is where fate and free will collide—it will tell you the struggles that you may have, but you may have the power to overcome those.

In Kundli matching, horoscopes of both the man and woman are compared to determine whether they match—this is done through matching ashta koota, considering 36 points in the different categories. Typically, a match of 18 or more implies a compatible match with over 21 preferred. On the other hand, under 18 may show that the two are fundamentally incompatible. This is especially important for arranged marriages or marriages where the two do not know each other well to determine the general compatibility of several key points. There are eight main factors that will be considered.

Varna: Mental compatibility

This shows whether the two people show general compatibility with basic personality and skills or abilities. It takes a look at four different personality types, as well as general work ethic, egos, and spiritual development. If both people have the same personality type, one point is awarded.

The areas of personality look at:

1. Intellect, philosophy, and spirituality
2. Leadership, defenders of society, courage, and decisiveness
3. Business-mindedness
4. Work ethic and accountability

Vashya: Power compatibility

This determines which partner is more likely to be dominant in the relationship. Each individual will have one of five different personality types that will help to understand and discern dominance as well as compatibility. Up to two points can be awarded here. These are:

1. Individualistic with a preference for personal control and opinion
2. Domineering and powerful
3. Subservient
4. Accepting of power within a smaller scope of influence
5. Balanced and quieter in asserting power

Tara: Health and general wellbeing

This takes a look at whether the two spouses will be healthy together, looking at general benefits toward wellbeing. It can also aid in looking at longevity and fortune in the future. This is either good or bad and is worth up to three points.

Yoni: Physical and sexual compatibility

This will help to determine whether two people are compatible both physically and sexually, while also helping to understand the love between the couple. It will help to show attraction and sexual fulfillment as well. It is typically considered by looking at the sexual tendencies of each person as having characteristics of certain animals. Those animals are then either naturally friendly or adversarial toward each other, with some being neutral. The score is based on how compatible the animals are, and there can be up to four points scored here. The animals that are used for this are:

- Buffalo (Mahisha)
- Cat (Marjara)
- Cow (Gow/Gau)
- Deer (Mriga)
- Dog (Shwana)
- Elephant (Gaja)
- Horse (Ashwa)
- Lion (Simha)
- Mongoose (Nakula).
- Monkey (Vanara)
- Rat (Mushaka)
- Serpent (Sarpa)
- Sheep (Mesha)
- Tiger (Vyaghra)

Grahamaitri: Progeny, affection, and harmony

This category is worth up to five points and is designed to paint a picture of the likelihood of having children, along with the mutual affection that you share with your partner. It will also look at how people tend to consider the way that they look at the world as well in hopes of being able to identify daily behaviors and tendencies. This should, ideally, help to show the compatibility in attitude with one another alongside the likelihood of children.

Gana: Worldview

This takes a look closely at how people view life. Typically, people will take one of three positions when it comes to understanding the world around them. This will be worth six points if both people are on the same plane. These are:

1. Living with a focus on spiritualism rather than in the moment or materialistic.
2. Living with a focus on balance between materialism and spiritualism
3. Living with a focus that is down to earth.

Bhakoot: Prosperity and love

This takes a look at how likely the two people are to become prosperous or happy. It can also influence longevity, the satisfaction in life and in the marriage, and in having children. This can be worth up to seven points.

Nadi: Lifeforce and health compatibility

This takes a look at how likely you and the other person are to have similar physical features. It takes a look at Ayurvedic doshas to determine how similar the two people's energies are and how well they resonate. Some believe that this also looks at spiritual compatibility as well and will determine if you and the other person are likely to live long lives together. This can be worth up to eight points.

VEDIC ASTROLOGY FOR SELF-AWARENESS

Another common use of Vedic astrology is to turn straight inward—it involves looking inward toward self-awareness in hopes of getting insight into one's mind and body. It will help you to become more self-aware, learning to see all sorts of personal information. Oftentimes, through learning to understand your horoscope, you can then begin to become more self-aware. Your reflections can relate right back to that horoscope.

When you begin to understand your horoscope, you can then begin to identify where you may be creating your own issues in life. The Planets will set out the course on life that you are on—they will tell you that you are prone to one thing or another, but ultimately, you can take the actions if you are informed to make the changes. If your Planets tell you that you are likely to be self-defeating or that you are going to be highly unhappy in life, you can begin to tackle that point. If you can do that, you can begin to change up how you choose to engage with yourself. By changing those actions and making new ones, keeping the identified problems that you have in mind, you can then become more capable of charting your future accordingly.

We all have patterns in our lives that are problematic. They are self-defeating—they are actions that we regularly take over and over again, and though we might do something slightly different, we will find that we are running into the same pattern over and over. Think of how you can make the same piece of pottery over and over again—you can change the paint on the outside, but it is the same piece of pottery at its core. This is how your behaviors work in your life, and if you learn to identify them, you can then begin to change up what you do and how you do it. In your life, you will do this as well. Some people are terrible in their love lives—they make the same mistakes over and over again. Maybe you've been cheated on by every ex you've had. If this is the case, it's time to look at *why*. What could you be doing to draw these people in?

When you can find the self-defeating pattern, you can look to your horoscope. Look at Venus. Look at the Seventh House. Are there problems there? Reflect upon them. Is the problem rooted in struggling to communicate well? Go to Mercury. When you are able to find the cause of your problems, you can then begin to change them up. You can figure out what the Planets say about you so that you can then begin to change that up and fix the problem that is at the root of everything. By doing so, you can then fix the problem and start to fix things. Remember, even when we looked at the Planets earlier in the book, you saw that even negatives could be fixed if the focus was shifted to the right lesson to learn. Through this self-awareness through Vedic astrology, you can work to fix these habits and better yourself.

CHAPTER 9:
VEDIC ASTROLOGY TODAY

Now, at this point, there is no denying just how far Vedic astrology has reached and how much impact it has had on the people of the world, before and now. However, it is time for us to take the time to look into what Vedic astrology does these days for us. We are going to take a close look at the modern usage scenarios for Vedic astrology in this chapter, while also taking the time to attempt to better understand how science approaches Vedic astrology. Lastly, we will take a look at a phenomenon that fought for its right in court to be presented as a degree path: Vedic Astrology degrees.

This chapter is meant to show you how, even today, this is a highly influential practice that many people around the world still believe in. This is not something that was left in ancient history—it continued on as an important tradition to an entire culture of people, who eventually spread it around the entire world. If you wanted to, you could go just about anywhere and still find people who believe. In fact, it is so imperative to modern life that in India, it is even taught in colleges and universities.

And with that said, let's take a look at how people tend to take this process of discerning the unknown and laying out lifetimes of information all in a neat row for easy translation and interpretation. It is shocking just how far this reaches—we've already discussed baby names and marital counseling in earlier chapters, but people refer to Vedic astrology for so much more than just that.

MODERN USES OF VEDIC ASTROLOGY

Though initially practiced in India, it is also highly accepted in the Western world, as well as by many Western astrologers across the world. Because it is more accurate, it is something that many people turn to regularly. In particular, there are Vedic astrologers across the world, and they are able to do so much for you. Modern Vedic astrologers are highly skilled and typically trained, or even given degrees, in the process of reading birth charts for people like you who may want to know what the world has in store for them. If you are in the position of talking to a Vedic astrologer at any point, you may find that you are in a position where you get to ask questions, learn about yourself, and begin to benefit greatly as you learn more about yourself than you thought was possible. You will be able to glimpse into your past, present, and future, all by having a trained professional to talk to.

Now, there are many calculators online that promise to provide you with a quick breakdown of your own birth chart and information in your horoscope and what it may mean. However, there is very little as accurate as having an actual person piecing together everything in front of you. Vedic astrology, when you go to a practitioner, can provide you with the tools that you will need to help you in life. The purpose is that you should be able to make decisions with all of the information that you could possibly need right in front of you, providing you with everything that will help you. The hope is that with this information, you should be able to make decisions that are informed and are the most beneficial to you that they could be. If you teach yourself to understand Vedic astrology (and you're in the right spot if you are doing so!), or if you find someone versed in understanding charts, you will find that you will know what to do, when to do it, and how to make it work for you, and because of that, you will be able to gently ease your way into situations.

Vedic astrology serves a very real purpose: It is meant to be both practical and also therapeutic at the same time. It is practical in the sense that it can greatly assist in figuring out what to do, when to do it, and how to make it work for you. However, if you find that you are stuck in life, or even hurting, you will find that this tool can help you to either better understand a situation, to reframe it, or even to ensure that you have a better way to approach in general to get better results. We all want to achieve happiness, and yet for so many, this can be difficult to ever actually achieve. Because of this, you must be able to find ways for yourself to push yourself forward, and Vedic astrology oftentimes offers those tips that will help you with exactly that.

Because there are so many different aspects to consider in Vedic astrology, from signs to Lunar mansions to aspects and everything else, the results that you get are highly individualized. This gives Vedic astrology this interesting balance between being universal in the sense that everyone can access it—we all have a time and place of birth, which is the bare minimum necessary to begin understanding your horoscope. However, the world is vastly different, constantly changing, and the skies are rarely ever the same, and certainly are not the same from the same position at any given time. This means that you will get highly personalized results from something that can be applied to literally anyone alive.

Modern people choose to use Vedic astrology when they are stuck. Typically, they will approach an astrologer when they find that they are at a breaking point or at a crossroads, and they don't know what to do next. It could be that they don't know which path to take, and they are unsure of how to make the decision. They could be sick of constantly trying and getting the same problematic result over and over again. No matter the reason, one thing is for sure: All of the answers are in the universe, and they are there for the understanding. You will get to receive individualized advice based upon your own personal karmic pattern, and that means that you will then be able to act accordingly.

Remember, your free will is yours to control, and not even karma can take that away from you. However, you must also be mindful that you will have natural tendencies that repeat over and over again. Because of that, you want to ensure that you are on the right path. You want to ensure that you have all of the information to help yourself choose accordingly. Some common, real-life situations in which people approach an astrologer include:

- Attempting to make sense of a major decision
- Attempting to understand a child's life patterns and potential future
- Choosing a career
- Deciding to plan a healthy pregnancy
- Deciding upon education
- Figuring out when to get married
- Finding insight about something that was painful in the past
- Handling finances
- Interest in moving
- Learning about a health issue and how likely healing is
- Planning a business venture
- Planning to purchase property
- Relationship compatibility

SCIENCE AND VEDIC ASTROLOGY

Scientists are quick to scorn Vedic astrology, but the truth is, there may be more to it than meets the eye. Let's first look at the arguments against Vedic astrology and why so many scientists choose to vehemently protest that it is something to trust or rely upon. Then, we will take the time to try to translate that into real understanding and figuring out whether it is accurate or not. The truth is, scientists in India tend to swear by Vedic astrology, while many others argue that there is no scientific basis.

Astrology has been repeatedly refuted by the scientific explanation. Without any clear explanation for how the universe works or the ability to look into the future, it is very quickly rejected and rebuked. Repeated testing has been done, and scientists say that despite the fact that the astrologers of the world use scientific components, such as looking at the movement of Planets and other astronomical influences, there is no way that the positions of the stars and Planets could potentially impact the people on Earth.

It is argued, according to the naysayers, that it is nothing but chance or the Barnum effect and that there are all sorts of situations in which predictions have been wrong on more than one occasion. However, people tend to ignore these. There were predictions, for example, that in 2000, during a point in which many Planets aligned closely, astrologers claimed that there would be catastrophes. An entire village in India fled their homes, fearing tidal waves would drown them. However, there were no tidal waves, and many of the Houses ended up being robbed.

Overall, scientists have rejected Vedic astrology time and time again, refusing to admit that it could possibly be on the right track to ensuring that readings are real or that the universe could reveal secrets of karma or how it works. However, despite that, there are other unexplainable truths that science fails to account for as well. Think of religion—science has attempted to refute it for years to no avail.

Astrology s quite similar to that in this regard—people believe in it, and those beliefs are powerful.

THE PLANETS AND PEOPLE—ARE THEY REALLY INFLUENTIAL?

People argue that there is no way for the Planets to have such a sway over the people in the world, but the truth is, there are potentially many ways that the Planets, the sun, and the Moon could interfere with people. Think about it—the Moon is responsible for controlling tides of water. The gravitational pull of the Moon is enough to impact the Earth's water. How far-fetched is it to assume that people, built of water, would also be impacted?

If you've ever asked around, you've probably heard stories from doctors and L&D nurses swearing up and down that truthfully, people are more likely to be born or hospitalized on nights or days of full Moons. They believe this entirely. There are even a few studies that have backed this up. Published in 1966 by Holly Shulman, there is a study that took a look that eh Moon's phases. It showed that when you break down births by the phase of the Moon, looking at full Moons, half Moons, and quarter Moons, more births happen around the full Moon than any other. Additionally, a study also by Shulman that occurred a few years prior to the aforementioned one showed that the most births, when breaking days into consecutive three-day periods, found that there were three days with the full Moon in the center, where births occurred more often.

Aside from those studies by Shulman, there have been other attempts to scientifically justify astrology. One such attempt relates astrology to science, comparing it with quantum physics into what was referred to as quantum astrology. This sought to take a look at the fact that because the universe is vibratory, we are now able to see that the entire universe is built upon vibrations that occur, only some of which (arguably an infinitesimally small portion) can be perceived by people on their own. However, the more that we learn, the more that we can begin to observe them. We've developed ways of infra and ultra perception. We can look at and understand the frequency events that happened years and years prior. We can see subatomic waveforms and particles that seem to deny the idea of anything potentially existing as a solid. We know that there are areas beyond what we can observe in the universe, and because of that, how can we possibly deny something because we cannot see it?

Additionally, we know that Planets have their own frequencies—these have been instrumented since Brahe in the mid-16th century, which were then mapped accurately with math by Kepler. That information provided us with the math necessary for gravity. All of this scientific information, our understanding as humans can come together in quantum mechanics. Waves do not exist separately—they exist together and create more waves. This means that if the Planets have their own frequencies, they would absolutely be creating more waves that would, in theory, reach us on Earth.

This brings us to the idea of applying quantum astrology as well. To understand this, first think of the idea that, to some degree, even if down to the cellular level, you can see the Hindu idea of reincarnation. Cells live, they die, and they are reborn through cellular reproduction. They are constantly replacing themselves. Consciously, we may be a bit more than that. However, the same still stands. We live. We die. We are reborn. With quantum astrology, we can address this point. We can start to understand this idea that we do not exist on our own and that our bodies will always create this idea. We can see that we are particles, but also waves.

The idea is effectively boiled down to the idea that when you look at your map, you can see the path of the Planets. The Planets create their waves. Their waves influence us. We have a reality that is influenced but not controlled by those waves.

ADVANCED VEDIC ASTROLOGY DEGREES

Though the scientific community has attempted to argue for years, astrology has won its position in some Indian universities. The argument for allowing this study in the universities was that Vedic astrology is critical to traditional and classical knowledge. Additionally, it was argued by India's University Grants Commission and the Ministry of Human Resource Development that Vedic astrology was a way of understanding our world around us. It provides a lens through which the world can be understood in real-time. It lets us understand the universe, as well.

This decision was taken to court back in 2001, but it was backed—the courses were allowed to stand, and even today, you can still find universities that will offer advanced degrees in astrology. There have been attempts to petition the Supreme Court of India to remove this, but they so far have dismissed it. They claim that astrology is not the promotion of religion, and as such, it should be free to continue.

There are attempts to create a national Vedic University, which would combine teachings of astrology alongside those of tantra, mantra, and yoga in order to create an entire course system that would be true to the Vedas. These degrees and diplomas are meant to teach individuals everything that they will need to know to understand how the process of Vedic astrology works. They are meant to look at the various celestial bodies, attempting to show how they can influence the lives of those on Earth. There is a large focus on the subjects, learning them theoretically and practically first before then discovering how they work spiritually to begin to show further how much they offer.

Up until 2000, though some courses could be taught, there were no degrees that were designed to provide a degree in Astrology. However, Shri Murli Manohar Joshi chose to command UGC to begin offering astrology as a degree course. As a result, there are now several different schools around the country of India that will offer these degrees. There are both

Bachelor's and Master's degrees available. If you are interested in these schools, all it takes I a simple search for Indian Bachelor's degrees in Vedic astrology or a search for Jyotisha. You will be able to find several schools that offer these degrees.

Additionally, you can also find several programs that are entirely digital these days that will help you to begin studying Vedic astrology. These are accessible from just about anywhere, and you will be able to get the ins and outs of everything that you will need to know if you want to be able to provide this information for yourself. Of course, if you want to learn Vedic astrology, you can also just hit the books and study hard—there is plenty of information there that can help you to become better-versed.

CHAPTER 10:
INTRODUCTION TO STARGAZING

At this point, we've taken a lot of time to consider just the birth chart in your own reading of Vedic astrology. However, there is more to it than just that—you must also be able to understand and identify what is known as transits. These are the movements of Planets in real-time. The Planets are always moving, and as such, they are constantly changing their positions in the sky. This means that you need to be able to understand how to read them yourself. Now, you could always just look up a guide for the night, or you could also go out and take a look at the night sky. No matter whether you want to do things the old fashioned way of looking to the sky yourself or use a guide, we are going to take the time to look at how to understand stargazing in this chapter. We will go over what stargazing is, how it works, and what you need to know when you look up at the sky in hopes of learning something new. We will go over how to identify planets from stars, as well as the difference between a constellation and the Zodiac and more.

Stargazing, whether for your own astrological purposes or even jut o enjoy some quiet, is something that you should know how to do for yourself. We're going to go over some of the most important parts of the sky that you will need to know and recognize, and we will look at how you can better understand what you are seeing.

Now, before you begin, you might ask if you need a telescope. One would be nice to have if you want to get a closer look. However, they can be quite expensive, and you have other options available to you. You could also choose to, for example, take a look at getting binoculars or even just choose to understand which Planets will be where when so that you can figure out which are which and how to begin understanding what you see above you.

The universe itself is massive—the Planets that you see will look much like the stars in the sky as well, but one thing is for sure: The stars are far, far bigger. Remember, all of the Planets rotate around the sun—they are drawn in and trapped by the gravity of the Sun, and that means that they cannot escape their orbit. They are significantly smaller than the sun, which, all things considered, is quite small compared to the size of the other stars that you can see in the sky above you. However, they are the same size because of the sheer distance between yourself and the Planets versus yourself and the stars. Think about it this way for a moment—light travels at the speed of light, which is roughly 186,282 miles per second. Theoretically, it travels faster than anything else, and light would be able to travel around the Earth nearly eight times in just one second. It takes roughly 1.5 seconds for light to travel from the Moon to Earth. It takes roughly 8 minutes for light to travel from the Sun to Earth. The nearest stars that you can see in the sky require four *years* to send the light all the way to you where you can see it. That is a substantial amount of time that you must acknowledge.

HOW TO STARGAZE

Before we begin delving into the rest of the material, let's first begin to look at stargazing itself. It's not as simple as just stepping outside and looking up toward the sky—there is more to it than just that, especially if you live in the city. If you are in the city, you are surrounded by light pollution, which is going to make it next to impossible for you to make out anything meaningful in the sky. The light pollution will drown out much of your view, and that can be a huge problem for most stargazers. Now, you might feel a bit intimidated by the idea of going out, especially if you find that you live in a city. Don't worry—all you need to do is find a patch of sky that's cleared of clouds and make sure that you find somewhere that is far from lights so that you will be able to see more. If you've never seen the night sky in sheer darkness, away from the blinding lights of a city, you'll be in for a treat—the sky is as nebulous and magnificent as you could possibly believe at night when there is no light to blot out the stars. All you have to do is get yourself out somewhere.

If you can't get yourself out of town, the next best thing is to get yourself up as high as possible above the light. If you can, you could go up to the roof of a tall building. However, heading out to the outskirts of town is generally preferred. Then, simply look up to the sky and let your eyes begin to adjust!

When you are gazing, then, it is as simple as learning the constellations. If you don't yet know them in your area, it can be a good idea to keep a sky map or an application on your phone on hand. Just remember that blue light is no good for being able to see the sky. Use red light or a blue light filter on your phone to prevent damaging your night vision when you look at your phone. There are plenty of free apps that you can download that will help you to better spot the stars in the sky, especially with the addition of the GPS function on your phone.

From there, it's as simple as just getting out there on clear nights so that you can see as much as possible. If you can't get out, you can even just look up at the sky from your window—you should still be able to see something. If you spend ample time outside looking at the sky, you'll notice that the stars appear to move across the sky—this is actually Earth rotating. Beyond that advice, just don't overthink things, and you will have a great time getting out there to see all of the stars above you. This is a great way for you to enjoy your time exploring the universe around you without ever having to set foot off the ground. With that aside, let's go over what you can expect to see in the sky as you gaze.

OBJECTS IN THE SKY

The next time that you are outside on a clear night consider looking up. What do you see? There will be darkness for sure—the night sky is nothing but dark. However, within that darkness, there will also be tiny pinpricks of light that you can look to as well. Some of those little pinpricks will be stars—in fact, most of them will be. You may be able to find the Planets amongst them if you are looking in the right spot as well, and that can be beneficial to you. You may be able to see little dots of light that slowly and steadily move across the sky—they are likely to be satellites that are orbiting the Earth. You may also see the occasional shooting star, or if you are in the right place at the right time, you might get to see other astronomical bodies of interest—there could be a comet, or there could be asteroids or a meteor. There could be the Milky Way galaxy or anything else.

The night sky is full of wonders, but if you don't know what you are looking at, many of the different things that you see may look exactly the same. You might not be able to tell the difference between whether you are looking at a star or a planet, and that's okay. However, it is good for you to know the difference if you ever intend to look to the sky to identify current transits of planets, constellations in the sky, or anything else. Keep in mind that you have many different resources available to you that you can make use of—these are likely to be highly beneficial to you if you know where you are looking, and those could be great for you if you choose to reach for them. They are great for learning the ropes, learning to decipher out the constellations, the Zodiac, and more.

Now, to begin, we will take some time to identify any of the objects that you are likely to see in the sky when you are heading out to stargaze. The sky is filled with all sorts of different objects. Of course, the most important in Vedic astrology are the Sun, Moon, the Inner Planets, and the stars around you. However, there are other things that you might

INTRODUCTION TO STARGAZING | 179

be able to spot up in space as well that could be great for you to identify.

Sun

The Sun needs little introduction. If you are stargazing, it probably won't be visible since you'll be out at night! However, this star is highly essential in Vedic astrology and therefore got an honorable mention.

Moon

The Moon, likewise, requires very little in the way of a proper introduction. It will probably be visible sometimes, but not always, and it will wane and wax between full and new Moons.

Planets

There are only five Planets that are really visible to the naked eye, and those five are usually mistaken for stars. You will be able to see Mercury, Venus, Mars, Jupiter, and Saturn if you know where to look. There is no coincidence that these are the five emphasized Planets in Vedic astrology—they are the only ones that you can see without equipment. Keep in mind that stars do not produce light on their own. They reflect back the light of the sun, much like how the Moon does, to create the shining bodies that you will see in the sky.

Stars

The rest of the little sparkly things that you are likely to find in the sky are stars. They are massive balls of gas that is burning. They are barely visible from Earth because of the fact that they are so far away. However, most of them are significantly larger than the sun, which is, all things considered, quite small by star standards.

Constellations

Constellations involve being able to find patterns in the stars that are visible. They are usually just stars that appear to be close together in the sky, and they may appear to travel together. There are nearly 90 constellations that are commonly recognized, and you will be able to track these with an app on your phone or a map that you can print and view.

Near-Atmospheric Phenomena

Though the name sounds fancy, these are really mostly just manmade equipment that is in the atmosphere. This would include planes, satellites, and the like, and will also encompass the idea of shooting stars as well. Shooting stars are just debris that has entered the atmosphere that burns up long before it hits the ground.

The galaxy

You can actually see a piece of our galaxy if you know where you are looking. The stars and nebulae beyond our solar system are visible through the Milky Way. To see this, you will be able to spot a long, almost cloudy stripe across the sky.

DISCERNING STARS AND PLANETS

Stars and Planets will both look like specks of light if you don't know what you are looking for. However, there are ways that you can tell them apart. Typically, you can figure out the difference between star and Planet just by looking at how they exist. Stars flicker and twinkle while Planets tend to remain entirely still with their light. The Planets will move about in the sky, so it is hard to pinpoint where they might be. Typically, people can identify the star Sirius, which is typically far brighter than many of the other stars that are visible. However, if there is a second point of light that is visible and brighter than Sirius, it must be a Planet. Usually, they will be either Jupiter or Venus. A bright point of stationary light near the setting or rising Sun may be Venus or Mercury, both of which are almost always found close to the sun.

The reason the stars twinkle while the Planets don't is really quite simple—it all comes down to the dirt. Stars are further away from Earth than the Planets, and because of that, there is far more dust and dirt that is obscuring them. Because of this, the light can become distorted. However, the Planets, being so much closer than the stars, tend to not be as shrouded in dirt and dust, and because of that, there are other problems that will have to be addressed. Effectively, the further away from the sky the object is, the more likely that it is to twinkle.

Additionally, you will find that stars do not move in relation to the other stars around them. This is why the constellations change positions in the sky but never actually change shape. As the stars move across the sky, they never actually move away. The only shift in the stars that you will see will come from Earth moving. However, the Planets will shift positions throughout the night sky. They move because they are in orbit just like Earth is, rotating around the Sun at different speeds. This gives them the appearance of wandering. They will pass through various constellations and space in the sky throughout the year

THE ZODIAC VS. CONSTELLATIONS

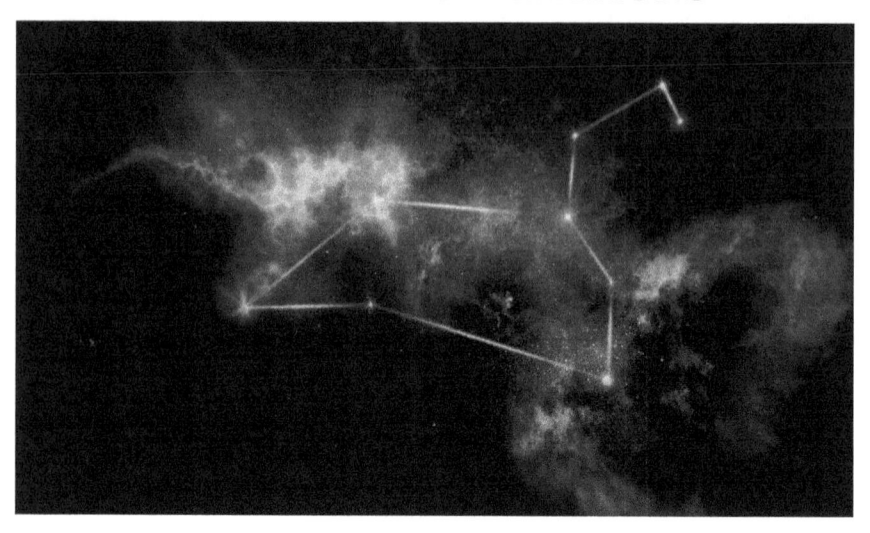

That brings us to the next point—the Zodiac versus constellations. Now, the Zodiac is built up of constellations—it is identified by the twelve constellations that exist upon its plane. However, the Zodiac itself refers to the space between the constellations—it is the sky's plane that has been separated into twelve different equal pieces as a way of telling the passage of time and space.

This is essential—the Earth, in its rotations, goes through all signs of the Zodiac throughout the year. Its ecliptic plane, the plane upon which the Earth orbits the Sun—is roughly the same as the other Planets. Most objects will orbit around the Sun in the same direction of Earth, creating the appearance of the Planets going through each of the constellations at different points of time. When the Planet appears to be in one of the constellations or Zodiac spaces, we refer to this as [planet] in [Zodiac sign]. This is essential to keep in mind—it shows that the Planets will always be within that plane that you will be able to interpret. Though you may not be able to see them at every single moment, they will fall somewhere within the Zodiac, and therefore, they can be interpreted. This is why, even if there are some Houses that are empty on one's natal chart, you will be able to identify them all somewhere, even if they are in the same House as other Planets.

Constellations are the various shapes that are made in the stars. While the Zodiacal signs themselves are constellations that are used to divide up the space in the sky, you can also find dozens of others that exist as well, typically all pertaining back to mythology at some point or another. These have been used for all sorts of purposes, from being able to navigate without maps and compasses to simply watching the passage of time.

GETTING STARTED

With those celestial bodies in mind, you will find that the natural starting point is to begin to familiarize yourself with the constellations, especially those of the Zodiac. These will be instrumental in your ability to stargaze, especially in the context of astrology. You will need to learn to discern which stars are constellations, which constellations are the Zodiacal signs, and which Planets you can see in the sky at any time. This takes practice and experience—the constellations may be memorable in shape, but the truth is, a truly dark sky is almost unbelievably jam-packed with stars. Most people don't realize just how truly filled up the skies can be; they are overwhelmed by the fact that they see the sky above in the sheer volume of stars that are present. This means that people have to be able to identify the fact that there are so many; they have to be willing to see just how busy the sky can get, and that can be a big problem for people. It can be tough to figure out which star is which, and though you can be shown dozens of charts, the only way to really identify them is through experience.

Alternatively, you can also just search the locations online—they are constantly being tracked and, therefore, easy to find in astronomy reports each day. They will not only give you a quick and easy guide to where everything is, but they will also tell you everything that you need to know to be able to locate everything that you are searching for. Once you know the locations of the Planets, you can begin to interpret them as well, which will give you plenty of information that you will then be able to use in your real life situations as well.

CHAPTER 11:
UTILIZING VEDIC ASTROLOGY

And now, let's take a look at how Vedic astrology can be utilized. It is a highly powerful system that can be used to get plenty of information, as we have discussed thus far. It is capable of providing so much information to people, and it is able to show people how their horoscope is going to impact them during that period of time. As you probably noticed reading through the earlier chapters, there are plenty of places at which you might realize that your star signs will have different impacts on you over time.

If you were to go to an astrologer for a reading, they would take a look at what is known as your transit chart—it would show you which Planets could be found in different Houses at that point in time and how that could correlate with your own birth chart as well. They go together, and you get your own unique reading. Remember, the Houses, though they rule the same aspects of life, will also House different Planets and Zodiacal signs based upon the natal chart, and that will go into how you can interpret your transit chart as well.

Within this chapter, we are going to take a look at how this all comes together to create the readings that you will have in Vedic astrology. We will first take a look at what the transits are in-depth and then begin looking at how they can be interpreted. Finally, we will see how to analyze the information that has been provided. While the birth chart will tell you about yourself intimately and will show you who you are as a person, it is how the Planets move beyond that point of birth that determines your experiences at the moment. You will need to be able to see this to understand your birth chart at any point other than the moment that you are in.

Now, let's get started with information about the transit charts and why they are so important.

TRANSIT CHARTS AND THE PLANETS

As implied, the transit is important because it marks where in the sky, and therefore where in the Zodiac your Planets are. This is necessary for you—it helps you to begin to see the impacts that each Planet is having over you at any point in time so that you can better understand what is going on. Each Planet has very different transit speeds and therefore have its own path that is taken across the sky. Each Planet will be influential in different ways.

This is where aspects come in as well—we have discussed aspects in passing here and there, but they are formed when the Planets form alliances with your birth chart. When the Planets transit through the birth chart, they make alliances or conflict with each other, strengthening or weakening the power of that particular Planet as it governs the world around you. Now, let's take a look at the transits of Planets before we get any deeper into this:

- **The Moon:** This travels throughout the entire chart in roughly 28 days, spending just 2.5 days per sign before moving on to the next one.

- **Mercury:** Mercury's transit is somewhat strange. It is closer to the Sun and, therefore, sometimes has some strange movement patterns. It tends to g retrograde often. It will take a year to get through the entire Zodiac, but the time that it spends in each sign varies between 14 and 30 days.

- **Venus:** Like Mercury, this sign tends to spend different periods of time in each sign as well. It spends anywhere between 23 days and 2 months in each sign.

- **Mars:** Mars is slower to move through the Zodiac. It takes roughly two years to get through all of the different signs, remaining in signs for roughly 1.5 months before moving in others. However, this is not guaranteed either—sometimes, it can get caught up in certain signs and remain there much longer.

- **Jupiter:** Jupiter takes its time to travel around the Zodiac, and because of that, it is recognized as being much more influential over one's circumstances than the inner Planets, which take far less time to travel around. Jupiter spends roughly 12 years traveling through the Zodiac sign, which translates to remaining in each sign for roughly a year at a time.

- **Saturn:** This Planet is the slowest of them all and will take 29.5 years to get through the Zodiac. Saturn remains in each sign for roughly 2.5 years before moving on and is also deemed to be highly influential.

- **Rahu and Ketu:** These two are always found moving in retrograde due to the nature of these celestial beings, and can be a bit tricky. They take roughly 1.5 years to get through each Zodiac.

ASPECTS AND TRANSIT

With those transits in mind, you can see that the Planets and signs are constantly moving throughout the Zodiac even if some of them are quite slow. Now, let's return to the idea of aspects. Aspects are the relationships that are formed between Planets or Zodiac signs based upon a comparison to your natal chart and the position of the Planets or signs that particular day. The Planetary aspects are referred to as *Graha Drishti*, and the sign aspects are called *Rasi Drishti*. We will need to look at both of these types of aspects can compare them to transit to get a better idea of what you need to understand.

Planetary aspects

Planetary aspects will occur when you have a Planet in a House that it does well in. Think about the strengths and weaknesses we discussed when going over the Planets earlier in the book—the strengths are good aspects while the weaknesses are the Houses that create a bad aspect. When a Planet is placed into a House that it is strong in, it is said to have a good aspect. Conversely, when a Planet travels into a House that it is weakened in, it is said to have a bad aspect. This can wreak havoc on one's life depending upon the Planet and position. However, there are other types of aspects as well that must be considered: Opposition, Trine, Square, and Sextile. Each of these will matter to you in different ways and are related to whether or not the Planets are friends, neutral, or enemies with each other.

1. **Opposition:** This refers to two Planets that have a difference of 180 degrees in their current placement. They are in opposite Houses. Rahu and Ketu are always in opposition. Effectively, to identify this, you will look at Planetary placements that are 7 Houses away. If you are looking at a Planet in your Ascendant, for example, it is in opposition with any Planets that are in your Seventh House. They are directly opposite each other and work like Yin and Yang. They are conflicting, but they must also cooperate together, and you must be able to find the balance between them.

2. **Trine:** This refers to Planets that are 120 degrees apart from each other, meaning that they are four Houses apart from each other. If you have a Planet in your Fourth House, it is in trine with Planets in your Eighth House, as well as within your Twelfth House in the opposite direction. Trines are typically considered positive because the energy is able to flow easily, and it is said to bring good luck and opportunity between those Planets in the areas of life that those Planets rule.

3. **Square:** This refers to Planets that are 90 degrees apart. When Planets are in square, they are three Houses away from each other. This means that you could have a square between the First and Fourth Houses. This is typically referred to as positive, and the angle can be responsible for some discontent, but that discontent is necessary to begin making progress. It is indicative of a challenge before success and the learning of an important lesson.

4. **Sextile:** Sextile Planets are those that are separated by just two Houses. Similar to trine, the sextile is indicative of talents and opportunities, but in this case, the talents that are being addressed are difficult—they require effort and skill to totally engage with, and that can be difficult to manage at times. However, it is well worth the effort, and success will be earned.

Those patterns become beneficial to understand—they can create aspects between Planets that are currently placed nearby each other on your natal chart. With those patterns in mind, consider the following relationships between the Planets as well:

Planet	Friends	Neutrals	Enemies
Sun	Moon, Mars, Jupiter	Mercury	Venus, Saturn
Moon	Sun, Mercury	Mars, Jupiter, Venus, Saturn	
Mercury	Sun, Venus	Mars, Jupiter, Saturn	Moon
Venus	Mercury, Saturn	Mars, Jupiter	Sun, Moon
Mars	Sun, Moon, Jupiter	Venus, Saturn	Mercury
Jupiter	Sun, Moon, Mars	Saturn	Mercury, Venus
Saturn	Mercury, Venus	Jupiter	Sun, Moon, Mars

Beyond just considering the relationships between the Planets, let's consider the Houses in which the Planets are able to be well aspected and those that tend to pose problems for them.

Planets	Good Aspect	Bad Aspect
Sun	1st, 5th, 9th, 10th	4th, 6th 7th, 8th, 12th
Moon	4th, 7th, 9th, 11th, 12th	2nd, 3rd, 6th, 8th
Mercury	1st, 3rd, 5th, 6th, 7th, 10th	2nd, 4th, 8th, 9th, 12th
Venus	1st, 2nd, 4th, 5th, 7th, 9th, 11th, 12th	3rd, 6th, 8th, 10th
Mars	1st, 3rd, 5th, 8th, 10th, 11th	2nd, 4th, 5th, 6th, 12th
Jupiter	5th, 7th, 9th	
Saturn	3rd, 6th, 7th, 10th, 11th	4th, 5th, 8th, 9th, 12th
Rahu	1st, 2nd, 3rd, 5th, 10th, 11th	4th, 6th, 7th, 8th, 9th, 12th
Ketu	4th, 6th, 8th, 9th, 12th	1st, 2nd, 3rd, 5th, 7th, 10th, 11th

The Planets, when in Houses they do well in, will create auspicious changes to your life. However, you will need to be careful when they are poorly aspected, as this can cause many problems related to that particular Planet and House.

Sign aspects

Of course, the signs can also be aspected as well. This might seem strange at first when you consider that they will never overlap, but remember, the aspect is created when something is moving in real-time crosses a specific position in your natal chart. Let's say that you have Aries in your Ascendant. If Leo, Scorpio, or Aquarius is in the First House, they will be aspected thanks to the relationship between them. Generally speaking, you can expect the following relationships with your Zodiacal signs:

Zodiacal Sign	Aspects
Aries	Leo, Scorpio, Aquarius
Cancer	Scorpio, Aquarius, Taurus
Libra	Aquarius, Taurus, Leo
Capricorn	Taurus, Leo, Scorpio
Taurus	Capricorn, Libra, Cancer
Leo	Aries, Capricorn, Libra
Scorpio	Cancer, Aries, Capricorn
Aquarius	Libra, Cancer, Aries
Gemini	Virgo, Sagittarius, Pisces
Virgo	Gemini, Pisces, Sagittarius
Sagittarius	Pisces, Gemini, Virgo
Pisces	Sagittarius, Virgo, Gemini

APPLYING THE INFORMATION

Now, it's time to start understanding how this all comes together. Transits, which we have been looking at in terms of aspects, are highly useful and are used widely throughout Vedic astrology. Transit, once again, will refer to the movements that the Planets make over time. Your natal chart is a quick snapshot of the sky at the moment of your birth, but the sky is constantly changing as well. That snapshot matters, but so does the current movement and alignment of the stars and Planets.

We look at transits primarily by looking at how the transiting Planets compare to our natal charts. We compare them to our chart to see where they fall and how they interact with the layout that we had at birth. As they move through the chart, they can either be neutral in effect, or they can have a positive or negative effect based upon the relationships with the Signs, Houses, and Planets that are presented on your natal chart. As the Planets transit, they bring new events and occurrences to our lives that are all related to fate and karma. They act out what was in store for us, and we then find ourselves trying to get through the interactions as well as individuals, in hopes of becoming capable of skillfully working through the event and understanding how it impacts us.

Typically, we care more about the slower Planets because they tend to have those longer effects on us. When the Moon changes signs every couple of days, it is constantly changing your life in much smaller amounts, but those transits that are longer, such as Saturn and Jupiter, tend to have much larger effects on us. We look to the Lunar transit to understand mood and emotions, but they don't do much more than that.

The Sun, Mercury, and Venus all tend to move roughly 1 degree per day, and in doing so, they tend to be more complex. They can make somewhat larger changes to one's life, and in doing so, they can trigger events that are related to changing up the bigger effects that we will see from the larger transits. Typically, these are really just glanced at in passing but are not used for in-depth understanding.

Mars is the first of the transits that actually becomes beneficial to look at. When you look at the transit of Mars, you start to see some useful information. This will show you how you choose to take action, and when you can see where Mars is on your transit, you can determine where in your life that you are about to get assertive. Mars lingers in Houses for a week or two, and because of that, you can turn to that House that Mars is in to start looking at the impact. Typically, Mars will help you to identify productivity and assertiveness in that particular aspect of your life, but you may also err on the side of aggression based on your chart and your actions that you take. If Mars is in your Seventh, you might find that you are focused on your relationship at the moment.

Jupiter is where things start to get interesting in your chart. Jupiter typically creates grandness. It is a positive sign, and it will usually highly influence the Houses that it is in, typically providing them with a boost of fortune. This auspicious sign tends to bring with it good feelings, and it can bring positivity to Houses for a month, or even longer if it finds itself slipping into retrograde. This is somewhere that is linked to current successes and positivity most of the time.

Saturn, on the other hand, is usually linked with negativity. Saturn itself, though not always bad, tends to carry an air of negativity with it Saturn will bring with it lessons that need to be learned and a reality check to the reading. If you are able to persevere and learn what you need to do, Saturn is linked to great strides in life and growing greatly as a person. If you are able to react well with your Saturn in mind, you can usually find that you benefit greatly. You will be rewarded, and that is well-deserved after the time spent trying to get through these processes. You must be able to see the ways that you can react with Saturn so that you will be able to learn those important life lessons that the universe is trying to teach you. While it typically transits for two months per sign, it can sometimes go retrograde and linger for up to six months at a time.

Sometimes, transits can interconnect— through single and double transits, when two are aligned, are not usually all that important, but sometimes, you can be hit with three transits at a time. These can become aspect patterns that are highly influential. Because the Planets are so closely related to each other, they are able to activate other Planets by their proximity. Sometimes, you can run into the activation of several Planets, and that can have very interesting effects on life in general. This is where you start to see the patterns, such as the ones listed earlier. You will have trines, squares, sextile, and opposition. However, there are some others that may be present as well. Remember, these are where the transits and the natal chart collide—they involve looking at both how the skies around you are influencing the world around you and at how that interacts with your own personal horoscope. Every person will have different ways that they feel the energy of the present sky based upon their individual birth charts. However, there are other ways that become important to consider, as well. Let's consider four more key points to consider when attempting to analyze the current transits.

Lordship of the transit Planet

We've looked at lordship of Planets already. It is highly important to recognize and understand. Remember, each Zodiac sign is lorded by a Planet, and that can create interactions when they are aligned. When you look at the lordships of the Planets, you can determine whether they are going to have good results or bad results. This is highly based upon compatibility with that particular lord. Consider whether the Planet that you are looking at is in a malefic or benefic house to determine this. If the lordship and the house are both auspicious with the Planet, then usually, you will have auspicious results. Conversely, if you have a Planet in a malefic house, then there will probably be problems.

Effects of the transit Planet

Next, you must consider the general effects of the Planet itself. Typically a Planet in a malefic house will create malevolent or unenjoyable effects while positive, benefic houses will create good results. Keep in mind that malefics, such as Saturn, Mars, Rahu, and Ketu, will show good results in the upachaya houses—the 3rd, 6th, and 11th. Effectively, you must double check the house along the transits as well to determine how likely you are to see good or bad results.

Ashtakvarga analysis of the transit Planet

You must also look at the Ashtakvarga analysis as well, which refers to a system in which auspicious impacts of a Planet are measured based on each other. Effectively, under this analysis, you want to consider the fact that when a Planet has more than four benefics, then that transit is much more likely to create a good effect, no matter what the position is. Jupiter is one such example—when Jupiter has more than four benefics at any given moment, it is going to have positive effects on its house that it is in, regardless of how likely they are to be good for each other.

Co-relation of the transit Planet to Mahadasha lord

Finally, you must look at the co-relation of the Planet's transit with the Mahadasha lord. This allows you to see more about the person—you will be able to look at whether they are going to be successful or not. You will need to look at their dasha and make sure that they are supportive. For example, imagine that you are looking at someone with a Pisces ascendant. He is in a Jupiter dasha for roughly 2.5 years, during which Jupiter is aligned well with its place on the birth chart. When this happens, there will be good times ahead.

Effectively, when you are considering transits, you will have to look at dasha as well. Then, you can combine them together. They will work together to create the entire image that you are trying to see, which will provide you with far more information than you thought that you would get, something that is highly important for you. If you want to be able to get this information accordingly, you will need to do so carefully. You will need to take the time to figure out what goes into the process, and you will need to practice applying it.

Now, this sounds like a lot—and it is. However, it is information that will become relevant to you as you continue to interpret and understand various readings, charts, and more. Over time, you will be able to identify the different aspects of Vedic astrology, and you will soon learn to start applying it to your own life, or even other people's as well.

CONCLUSION

No matter where you are on Earth, one thing is true: The same sky will always be above you. The same sky will be there for every single person on this Earth. We will all see the same stars, the same Planets, and the same Zodiac. We will all be ruled by these great heavenly bodies above us. However, despite the fact that your sky and the sky of the person next to you are identical, the fact that the skies were different at the moment of your births matters. Though we all live under the same sky, see the same stars and Planets, and acknowledge that we can understand them, the truth is that our lives are all vastly different from one another.

Karma has a way of changing everything for each person. It will create vastly different circumstances for each person. One person might be born in a happy life, with happy friends and grow to be moderately well off. The next might be born in poverty. Though two people can be born on the same day, if they are born at different times or places, their skies on the horizon are different, and that changes everything about them, their lives, and more. Karma will be back to provide them what they have sown. Karma will teach people the lessons that they still must learn one way or another, and that lesson will be written in the stars upon the moment of birth.

You've now begun to scratch the surface into understanding the basics of Vedic astrology. The truth is, this is a method that can tell you the innermost secrets that you need to learn. It will help you to see your own cosmic balance sheet all in one spot so that you can begin to make the necessary adjustments. You will see the karma that is still maturing, the karma that you will reap, and even the karma that you are likely to make, all in one spot, laid out on your birth chart. This means that you can look to your chart for guidance so that you can begin to figure out what the universe has in store for you.

Millions upon millions of people have used Vedic astrology to look to their fates. They have used this to help to identify their personalities, their tendencies, their fates, and more. It is great to aid in providing this feedback, and we've gone over this in depth at this point in time. Despite the depth that we have taken, however, you have still only been introduced to the basics. There is so much to learn that entire classes and degrees can be founded upon learning to understand how the positions of the stars and Planets can dictate everything. You just have to learn to open your eyes to them.

Remember, as this book comes to a close, you can begin to apply this information. If you are stuck in your life at any point in time, taking a look at your horoscope is a great way for you to begin to identify why or how you could be. This is the perfect way to begin to get that insight that you need in life. Are you stuck because you are caught up by your planetary array? Is there something about yourself that you may have overlooked? Look to your Ascendant—what does it say about you? Are you stuck in your marriage? Take a look at your Seventh House and Venus's placement to determine if there is something larger than yourself going on. There is so much information that you can glean from looking to the stars. There is so much that you can learn about the universe and your karma. All you have to do is look up. If you can do that, you can begin to make sense of the world around you.

Now, if you are getting ready to start applying this information after you have read through the entire book, the first starting point is to get your birth chart. All you will need for this is your date and time of birth, as well as the place. If you have that, you can see exactly what the sky looked like to you as you entered the world. You will then be able to understand your Ascendant, which is the most influential part of the entire horoscope. Take a look at what your Ascendant sign and your Ascendant Planets are, if you have one, and let that information help you to figure out more about yourself. With time, you will come to discover far more about yourself than you thought you could know. Let yourself come to accept the information that you read and then try to let that guide you.

You are likely to find that a lot of the information that you read will resonate with you as you look at your birth chart and start to look at the information that was provided in the book. When you do this, reflect upon the information that you have gotten and start to think about how it will influence your life. This is simple—it will provide you with plenty of information that you will be able to look at.

When it comes to looking at other aspects of your life, such as your relationships that you have with the people around you, the way that you engage with your family, and your career, you can begin to get information as well. Look to your Ascendant sign and Planet for more information about these, as well as to the Houses that preside over these factors. With effort, you should start to see what you need to do and how you can come to expect everything to work out for you. All you have to do is ensure that you are in a position of knowing what is going on and what your signs are, and you will begin to be able to put it all together.

Remember, this information is fate, but you still have the power of free will over it. Though the fates have spoken, there is still plenty that you can do. When you look to this accordingly, you will be able to determine so much more about your life and what you need to do. Take action. Be informed by learning how your fates and the Planets will dictate your life and live your best life with those constraints. Every sign has the potential for great growth and development if you know what you are doing. Every sign can show you that you can learn your karmic lessons and better yourself. You just have to make sure that you go out of your way to do so and to go through the efforts of trying to better yourself.

Think of Vedic astrology as your tools as you navigate the world—as a map that you can rely upon to ensure that you know what you are doing and how to do it. When you do this, you will be able to better yourself and those around you. Remember, just as the Planets influence you, they also influence those around you—the influence that they have over you can extend to certain people depending upon the relationship that you have, and that means that you need to be able to acknowledge this. You must be able to recognize the changes and effects that the Planets and stars will have over your relationships, from your spouse to family and even friends and business associates. Everything will be impacted because everything in this universe is interconnected, and the sooner that you make use of this, the sooner that you will realize that you are on track for those necessary changes in your life.

Vedic astrology will tell you what you need to know, and you will then be able to make use of it. However, there is more to it than what is even provided here. There are other aspects that can continue to influence you if you chose to delve in further, such as taking a look at how you can understand the Yogas—the organization of the planets in the particular patterns that you can see. You can learn to see other ideas and truths as well.

From here, consider delving deeper into Vedic astrology to get more of an idea of what it ought to be. Take a look at some ancient astrology books. Read some of those initial holy texts. You may choose to read into each of the different aspects of Vedic astrology in even more depth. There are entire books that could be written about each and every aspect of Vedic astrology, and this book has just scratched the surface. You can begin to look to the Lunar Mansions, looking into the myths and meanings. You can look at the Lunar nodes, the Planets, and more. Consider also taking the time to go out and stargaze at this point as well—learn what the Universe has to provide you and see the way that you can interact with everything. These are highly important ways for you to begin to connect to the Planets, the Universe, and to begin to open your mind more. Consider cracking open the *Parasara Hora Shastra*—that first text about Vedic astrology that was mentioned in Chapter 2. There are all sorts of places for you to turn in your studies. You just have to choose where to go next.

Thank you for taking the time to read through this book—you have been provided plenty of information that can help you to begin deciphering your horoscope and to look into the power of the Universe. If you've found the information in this book to be useful, informative, and enjoyable, please consider heading over to Amazon to leave a review. Good luck, and may the stars and Planets align in your favor!

DESCRIPTION

Have you always wondered why your life tends to go in the same patterns over and over again? Have you been trying to escape from the same old patterns, year after year, to no avail? If so, then keep reading... You may need Vedic astrology to begin deciphering your life.

Vedic astrology dictates that everything that you do in life is influenced by the positions of the stars and Plancts at the moment of your birth. It asserts that you are born according to karmic justice and judgment and that karma is written out into the stars at that exact moment. For this reason, people have turned to the skies for thousands upon thousands of years to begin to decipher the karmic workings and understand why their lives work the way that they do.

Karma is the sum of your actions in this life and in past lives, all of which is designed to bring you closer to liberation—that point in your life where you are able to become connected to the Universe and freed from the endless cycle of rebirth and death that we live in. It is something that you can never escape as it is simply the sum and reaction of your actions—it happens whether good or bad, and you will have to deal with the aftermath either way. However, karma brings with it lessons that are designed to help you achieve that liberation in life.

Because karma can influence every aspect of your life and because it is written in the stars, you can begin to understand why you go through what you experience and how likely that you are to succeed or fail in all sorts of aspects of your life. You just have to open up your mind, look to your birth chart, and begin to interpret it. This has been used for thousands of years to determine matchmaking, success, business ventures, and more. It helps us to understand how we experience the world around us and why it is the way that it is. It shows us our relationships with others, our friendships, and our shortcomings. It shows us our career prospects and health. There is so much about the world that can be read in the stars, so long as you know where to look. This book is here to help. It is here to teach you the basics of Vedic astrology so that you can begin to decipher the world around you and what fate has in store for you. In particular, you will find:

- Information on what Vedic astrology is and how it differs from Western astrology
- A brief history of Vedic astrology
- The Vedic birth chart and how you can begin to read it to start interpreting your own horoscope
- The role of the Planets and how to understand them in Vedic astrology
- The role of the Zodiacal signs and how they must be interpreted
- The role of the Houses and how they influence everything, as well as what happens when each Planet is found in each House
- The various Lunar Mansions and how they are influential over the individual
- The significance of Vedic astrology and how it is used to change people's approaches to life
- What Vedic astrology has become today
- How to stargaze and how to use that stargazing in Vedic astrology
- *And more!!*

Don't spend another day leaving life to chance. You can take charge and learn why you experience what you experience, and more. All you have to do is make it a point to get started today. Scroll up and click on BUY NOW to begin discovering the secrets of the universe.

CPSIA information can be obtained
at www.ICGtesting.com
Printed in the USA
BVHW050941041120
592494BV00016B/1076